THE GE[EK]
GUI[DE]

PERSONAL FINANCE

CRANE HILL
PUBLISHERS

The Geek's Guide to Personal Finance

ISBN-13: 978-1-57587-253-7
ISBN-10: 1-57587-253-6

Design by Miles G. Parsons

Printed in the United States

Library of Congress Cataloging-in-Publication Data

Ivey, Allison.
   Geek's guide to personal finance / by Allison Ivey.
     p. cm.
   ISBN-13: 978-1-57587-253-7
   1. Finance, Personal.   I. Title.
  HG179.I945 2006
  332.024--dc22

2006031092

THE GEEK'S GUIDE

PERSONAL FINANCE

Allison Ivey

CRANE HILL
PUBLISHERS

CONTENTS

Dollars and Sense.. 7

Straightening Out Your Stuff 9

Taking the Mystery Out of Your Credit History 23

Blueprint for a Budget... 37

The Power and Pitfalls of Plastic 47

Checklist for Checking Accounts.............................. 61

The Necessity of Nest Eggs 73

Supporting Your Uncle Sam 83

Getting Wheels Without Being Taken for a Ride 93

Hunting for Hearth and Home 109

Policies for Staying Healthy, Wealthy, and Wise 127

Dealing With Disability... 141

Leaving Something When You Go 151

Covering Your Assets 163

Gearing Up for the Golden Years 171

Having the Last Word 181

Index 187

THE GEEK'S GUIDE

DOLLARS AND SENSE

I've always heard that failing to plan is planning to fail. That is especially true when it comes to personal finances. You have to work to get everything in shape and keep it that way. Then, when change becomes necessary—when you need a new car, a new place to live, or a new savings account—you can make smart moves. Planning ahead, setting goals, and learning some basic management and organizational tools are a must to keep your financial life running smoothly.

I hope this book enables you to achieve your goals, and helps you be the most prosperous geek you can be.

STRAIGHTENING OUT YOUR STUFF

The first step to getting your finances in order is to get your financial records and papers organized. This can help you literally see your status on paper, and can also help you avoid financial headaches.

Getting organized can help you pay your bills on time (and avoid late payments), recognize immediately when charges are incorrectly made to your accounts, and more importantly, let you know if you're the victim of fraud or identity theft.

You'll need a place set aside just for handling your business where you can get organized. This place can be a home office, a kitchen table, or a spot in your basement, just as long as you have room for a few basic supplies.

Equipment and Supplies You Will Need

There are a few basic pieces of equipment and supplies you'll need as you get started.

- File cabinet: You need a place to file important papers, statements, and receipts for easy access. Have plenty of folders, and assign one to each type of information you need to save.

- Computer: Most people need a computer to keep track of their accounts, handle e-mail, and pay bills online. If you don't want or need a computer, you will have to handle everything on paper and by phone or mail.

- Calculator: Whether you use the one on your computer or have an abacus, you'll need one. You don't have enough fingers.

- Stapler and staple remover

- Tape dispenser and tape

- Garbage can

- Recycle bin (if recycling is available)

- Shredder

- Paper clips

- Calendar

- Bulletin board

An **abacus** is a calculation tool that was developed between 2400 and 300 BCE. It is often constructed of a wooden frame with beads sliding on wires, and is still widely used by merchants in the People's Republic of China, among other places.

 *Getting organized is the first step to getting your financial affairs in order.*

Information You Should Keep

There are important papers that should be organized and kept for easy reference. So what are they? Here's a list of common documents that most people need to keep handy.

- Checking and savings accounts – a record of account numbers, individual and joint, plus copies of monthly statements. Make sure you have documentation for accounts in the name of minor children, too.

- Retirement accounts – keep a record of account numbers and statements for IRAs and 401(k), 403(b), and 457 plans.

- Non-retirement accounts – this will include information about investments other than those related to retirement.

- Personal information – store copies of birth certificates, Social Security card information, passport information, marriage certificate, wills, and any other important documents.

- Credit card accounts – include account numbers, plus copies of monthly statements. This should include gas and store credit cards.

GEEKOID

Many people find it helpful to designate two days a month for paying bills, and then do so only on those days. That way, you have a regular date to take care of everything instead of worrying about it every day. Mark the dates you choose on your calendar so you remember to take care of this important job.

GEEKOID

A shredder can be a vital tool in preventing identity theft by getting rid of old documents that contain vital information such as account numbers, your Social Security number, and even your date of birth.

- Home mortgage papers – copies of your mortgage agreement should be included, plus any supporting paperwork you received at the time of purchase. If you rent a home or apartment, make sure you have a copy of your lease.

- Insurance information – copies of policies for home, auto, life, and even papers on minimal policies provided by certain organizations as a benefit of membership.

- Outstanding loans – paperwork and payment books for student loans, auto loans, and other monies you are repaying.

- Tax returns – copies of every state and federal tax return you file. Even if you file electronically, print out a hard copy for your records.

- Wills and trusts – updated wills, trusts, plus papers regarding powers of attorney. This may also include copies of a living will, or copies of other people's wills that list you as the executor or beneficiary.

 *Be sure to keep important papers on hand until you no longer need them.*

GEEKOID

If you have access to your accounts online, you probably have passwords to access them. Several accounts at the same institution may be linked to a common password, but accounts at different locations will have different passwords. Record all your passwords, especially the ones you may forget if you don't use them frequently, and keep a copy of the record separate from the account information for security purposes.

How Long You Should Keep Stuff

Once you've filed all your records appropriately, you may wonder how long you'll need to keep everything. Here are some general guides for that.

- Taxes – seven years or permanently. The IRS has three years from your filing date to audit your return if it suspects good faith errors, and seven years if it thinks you underreported your gross income by 25 percent or more. So keep tax returns and all documentation for seven years from the time of filing, but keep the actual return and proof of payment or refund permanently. There is no time limit on when the IRS can come after someone who fails to file a return or files one that is deemed false or fraudulent. The audit, admonishes the IRS, can begin "at any time." So keep a copy of your return as proof you filed.

- IRA contributions – keep permanently.

GUERRILLA GEEK

Be sure to guard your Social Security number just as securely as your credit card numbers. It is valuable loot for identity thieves. If someone has used your Social Security Number fraudulently, and you have done all you can to fix the problem without success, the Social Security Administration may assign you a new number. However, they cannot guarantee that a new number will solve your problem.

You *cannot* get a new Social Security number if:

- you have filed for bankruptcy.
- you intend to avoid the law or your legal responsibility.
- your Social Security card is lost or stolen, but there is no evidence that someone is using your number.

Contact information for the Social Security Administration:
(800) 772-1213
TTY (800) 325-0778
www.ssa.gov

- Retirement or savings plan statements – from one year to permanently. Keep the quarterly statements until you receive your annual summary; keep the annual summaries until you retire or close the account.

- Bank records – from one year to permanently. Throw away checks or imprints of checks that have no long-term importance, but keep checks related to your taxes, business expenses, and housing and mortgage payments.

- Brokerage statements – until you sell your securities.

- Bills – from one year to permanently. In most cases, when you receive the canceled check and the next bill showing a payment was applied, the last bill can be tossed. Some people like to keep their utility bills for a year to see what they are spending each year. The power and gas companies will usually provide this upon request. You should keep bills for big purchases (jewelry, appliances, cars, collectibles, etc.) for proof of their value in the event of loss or damage.

GUERRILLA GEEK

While many people like to keep important papers such as life insurance and burial policies in a safe deposit box, it may be better to keep those at home where they can be located immediately in an emergency.

GEEKOID

The first Social Security number was issued sometime mid-November 1936. It is unknown what the exact date was, what the first number issued was, or to whom it was issued. That is because hundreds of thousands of cards were issued on or just before the first official day of this system, which was November 24, 1936.

15

GEEKOID

Remember that if something should happen to you, the executor of your will will need access to all accounts, deposit boxes, and information about where your assets are held. Be sure you create a detailed list of all your accounts, including user names, passwords or PINs, and combination and/or security codes to facilitate access.

- Credit card receipts and statements – from forty-five days to seven years. Keep the statements seven years if they document tax-related expenses.

- Paycheck stubs – one year. If your W-2 form and your 401(k) or other retirement contribution statements match your stubs, you can toss the stubs.

- House or condominium records and receipts – from six years to permanently. You get the first $250,000 of capital gains free of taxes ($500,000 for married filing jointly). You need to keep receipts that document expenses that lower your capital gains on each house you sell. This is a cumulative exemption, meaning that this includes all houses you own during your lifetime.

Staying Organized

Now that you have a place for everything, and everything's in its place, there are things you can do to maintain your new system.

RECORD	WHERE TO KEEP IT	HOW LONG TO KEEP IT
Birth, marriage, and death certificates	Safe deposit box or fireproof home storage	Permanently
Motor vehicle titles, purchase receipts	Safe deposit box	Duration of ownership
Canceled checks (nondeductible expenditures)	Home storage	Minimum of three years
Canceled checks (tax-deductible expenditures)	Home storage	Minimum of seven years
Tax returns	Home storage	Minimum of seven years

- At least once a week, sit down with all your mail and sort through it. That means you only handle it once.

- Recycle or throw away any junk mail and anything else you don't need.

- Shred any credit card offers or other mail that contains confidential information.

- Pay all bills. If they aren't due for a while, get them ready to go and write the due date on the back so you know when to mail them.

- Record any checks written or online bills paid in your check register right away to keep your balance up to date.

- File all paperwork for paid bills.

GEEKOID

People often get annoyed with the avalanche of unsolicited credit card applications that clutter up their mailboxes and desks. Some recipients are tempted to return the application with their pet's name, or even something creative like Elmer Fudd. But this prank took a unique turn recently when a West Hollywood realtor tried and failed to stem the tide of the applications by simply asking the companies to take his name off their lists. Finally, he tried a new approach: He scrawled across the application, "Never waste a tree," meaning that the company should not waste more trees making paper to send applications to him. In return, he received a credit card issued to "Never Waste Tree." The bank that sent it shall remain nameless in an effort to protect the careless.

- Before filing any statements for checking or savings accounts, retirement plans, or stock accounts, make sure the activity for the previous month matches your records. Filing these without double checking the figures can cost a lot of money.

- Get rid of clutter. Mess makes it harder to do the simple tasks that need to be done.

GEEKOID

The phrase "Have a place for everything, and keep everything in its proper place." is an oldie, but a goodie, and it still works today. Its first documented use was in an 1827 publication called "Neatness" by Reverend C.A. Goodrich.

- Never handle a piece of paper more than once. Avoid the "I'll just put this here for now" habit. Do what needs to be done, and be done with it.

- Follow through with every piece of paper that reaches you and put it in its proper place—not just back in the pile.

- Don't keep business cards tucked away in a drawer. Enter them into a contact manager database and then throw out the card. Or put the cards in a Rolodex on your desktop.

GUERRILLA GEEK

The Rolodex is a rotating file device that holds small blank cards on which contact information is written. Because the cards are the size of standard business cards, it offers the convenient option of inserting a business card into the file instead of rewriting contact information on a blank card. The name Rolodex is a combination of the words Rolling and Index. It was invented in 1958 by Arnold Neustadter, who also made life easier with these other inventions:

- Autodex – phone directory book that automatically opens to the right letter.
- Swivodex – an inkwell that does not spill.
- Punchodex – a paper hole puncher.
- Clipodex – a stenographer's aid that attaches to the knee.

GEEKOID

Many people find that online banking is a great way to cut the clutter. Almost every financial transaction or bank activity that you need can be done electronically, including bill paying. Obvious exceptions would be check deposits and cash withdrawals. But the service allows you to handle most banking transactions at your convenience on a 24/7 basis.

- As you make purchases, put all your receipts in a small envelope. Sort through them every month or every quarter. Check them against your debit/credit card statement if applicable, then either trash or file.

- Throw out last month's copy of a magazine when this month's copy arrives. If you must save issues, only keep a year's worth.

- Cancel subscriptions to magazines you don't read. Stop saving newspapers you will never have time to read.

- Eliminate places for paper to accumulate. Limit your stacking trays to three: one for incoming papers, one for things on hold, and the other for things to be filed.

Working a little every day to stay organized will take less time than getting straightened out once everything is a big mess.

• Have as few credit cards and bank accounts as possible. Lots of accounts mean more fuss and more stress.

Now you're ready to get your personal finances in shape.

GEEK AT A GLANCE

• Getting organized is an important first step in getting your finances in order.

• Set up a space to manage your finances.

• Gather important documents and records to be organized.

• Prepare folders for each type of information to be saved.

• Stay organized by going through your mail and other paperwork once a week, discarding what you know you don't need.

• Spend some time weekly updating files and discarding unnecessary papers to keep your workplace organized.

TAKING THE MYSTERY OUT OF YOUR CREDIT HISTORY

Possibly the most important and most basic tool for getting your personal finances in order is your credit report. This is a collection of information that tells your history of paying your bills, your current monthly debts, and other information that indicates how good a credit risk you are.

The information in a credit report is collected by credit bureaus, which specialize in gathering it and making it available to potential creditors. The report itself doesn't say whether you are a good risk. Rather, it provides information that can help others make that decision for themselves.

One way they'll do this is to look at your credit score, a three-digit number that takes into account and rates all the information on your credit report. These numbers range from 300 to 850, with the higher number indicting a better credit risk.

GEEK GLOSSARY

A **credit report** is a summary of your bill-paying history, what your monthly debts are, how much credit you have available, and any other information that can help a potential lender decide whether you are a good or poor credit risk.

How is Your Credit Scored?

Your FICO® score is the score lenders use most often when qualifying you for credit. Another company that provides scoring is Beacon. While FICO® and most other companies won't release the exact method used for scoring, here's what usually goes into it:

- Payment history (35%)

- Amounts owed (30%)

- Length of credit history (15%)

- New credit (10%)

- Types of credit used (10%)

GEEK GLOSSARY

Credit reputation is a term used interchangeably with the terms credit history and credit score.

Other factors include the number and type of inquiries, and public records, including bankruptcy filings. If you have an exorbitant number of new credit inquiries, this will affect your score, because it looks like you're preparing to get lots of new loans, meaning you're about to go into more debt. Inquiries for the purpose of getting a mortgage are the only ones that do not affect your credit score in the same way. All mortgage inquiries within a thirty-day period count as one inquiry. This was designed so that you can shop for mortgage rates and not be penalized.

 *Knowing what's in your credit report is an important step in assessing your financial status.*

How Your Credit Score Is Used

Your credit score is used in a variety of ways. Banks and other financial organizations use it to help them decide if they'll lend you money. Insurance companies use it to decide if you're a good, solid risk, and many employers

FICO® is an acronym for Fair Isaac and Company, who came up with the scoring formula that most creditors use.

even use it to decide if they'll hire you. In other words, it's difficult to get credit, insurance, a job, and even a checking account if you have bad credit. At the very least, you'll pay a higher interest rate for credit than consumers with a good credit score.

 *It's difficult to get credit, insurance, a job, and even a checking account if you have bad credit.*

How to Get a Copy of Your Credit Report

So if your credit report is that important, how do you get a copy and see what's in it, good or bad?

The median FICO® score America is 723.

GEEKOID

Generally, you will have a good credit score if you make all your payments on time, have a mortgage, one or two car loans, and only a few credit cards.

GEEKOID

Prospective employers very often run credit checks as a means to verify information provided by the applicant, as well as to find out information the applicant might not volunteer. A recent survey indicated that most employers request a credit check to see if the candidate is responsible (as indicated by how he or she pays bills), to verify employment history, and to determine the likelihood for workplace theft.

Thanks to a recent amendment to the federal Fair Credit Reporting Act, you can now get a free copy of your credit report from each of the three credit reporting agencies once every twelve months, upon request. You may do so by contacting the Annual Credit Report Request Service. The contact info is:

- Website: www.annualcreditreport.com

- Toll-Free Number: 877-322-8228

- Mail: Annual Credit Report Request Service, P.O. Box 105281, Atlanta, Georgia, 30348-5281.

 *Don't fall for ads from other sources claiming they'll give you a free credit report. Most of those companies are trying to sell you something.*

GUERRILLA GEEK

Here's an example, taken from FICO's website that illustrates how a poor credit score can hurt you. Using a $150,000 30-year, fixed-rate mortgage, here's a comparison of how much you'll pay for your mortgage if you have a good credit rating, as opposed to a poor one.

Your FICO® Score	Your interest rate	Your monthly payment
760 – 850	5.46%	$848
700 – 759	5.68%	$869
680 – 699	5.86%	$885
660 – 679	6.07%	$906
640 – 659	6.5%	$948
620 – 639	7.05%	$1,003

Having bad credit could cost you as much as $150 more a month for a mortgage, if you can get one.

You can get a copy of your credit report by paying a fee at any time and as frequently as you want by going to one of the three agencies' websites, by calling their toll-free number, or by sending your request through the mail. To purchase a copy of your credit report, contact one of the three following agencies:

Equifax
www.equifax.com
800-685-1111

GUERRILLA GEEK

Opinions differ on whether it's best to get a copy from all three of your credit reports at once, or spread the them out over the year. The reason some people think it's best to get them all at once is that you'll know right away if one or more of them has incorrect information, and you can clear it up. The reasoning behind spreading them out is that you can keep a check throughout the year on identity theft issues. If someone opens an account in your name the month after you requested all three, you may not find out for eleven months. For this reason, I personally feel that it's better to spread them out. You may want to request all three initially, and then after twelve months, start spreading the requests out.

Trans Union
www.transunion.com
800-916-8800

Experian
www.experian.com
888-397-3742 (888-EXPERIAN)

You are always allowed a free copy of a credit report directly from one of the three major agencies if you've recently been turned down for credit, insurance, or employment based on your credit score. The company turning you down must notify you of which agency provided the information.

You can also get a free copy of your credit report if you have had an incident of identity theft. Under any of these situations, you have sixty days from the time of the adverse report in which to request your free copy.

Once you are satisfied that your report is accurate, you should review your credit reports thoroughly once a year, checking to make sure any closed accounts are showing up as closed and paid off, and to make sure there are no errors, such as accounts that don't belong to you. If you find errors, report them immediately to the appropriate credit bureau. Each report should contain information on how to report inaccuracies.

GEEKSpeak:

"Credit cards are very dangerous. Every time I try to use one somebody starts chasing me with scissors."

J. Bothne

What You'll Find on Your Credit Report

Remember that each of the three agencies may have different information. While most major accounts, like a mortgage or a car loan, should be on all three, some of the smaller financial institutions report information to only one or two of the agencies.

Each late payment to your creditors lowers your credit score more than the previous one. So even if you're late with a payment, go ahead and make it as soon as possible.

Here are some items you can expect to find on your credit report.

- Identifying information: your name, nicknames, current and previous addresses, Social Security number, date of birth, and current and previous employers. This may also include phone numbers.

GEEKSpeak:

"Economy is half the battle of life; it is not so hard to earn money as to spend it well."

C.H. Spurgeon

- Credit information: specific information about each account such as the date opened, credit limit or loan amount, balance, monthly payment, and payment pattern during the past several years. When you repay a loan, the financial institution reports regularly how you are making your payments. They report if you are making your payments on time, thirty days late, sixty days late, or ninety days late.

  Each late payment on your record lowers your credit score more than the previous one. So if you're thirty days late on a payment, it is better to go ahead and make the payment as soon as possible, before it goes to sixty days. After ninety days a late payment becomes a judgment, and that will be indicated. A bankruptcy is also reported, and impacts your credit score greatly, making it almost impossible to get a loan.

  Information about your payment history remains in your credit report for up to seven years. Information from public records such as bankruptcies can remain in your report for up to ten years.

- Public record information: federal district bankruptcy records, state and county court records, tax liens and monetary judgments; and, in some states, overdue child support.

- Inquiries: the names of those who obtained a copy of your credit report for any reason. This information comes from the credit reporting agency, and it remains up to two years, consistent with federal law.

    Inquiries that you authorized are visible to anyone requesting a copy of your credit report. Inquiries by unauthorized companies like credit card companies who get only a partial credit report for the purpose of pre-qualifying you for a credit card can be seen only by you. These do not count against your credit score.

Here are some things that won't be found on your credit report:

- Income
- Bank account balances
- Race
- Religion
- Health (even if medical bills show up as debts)
- Criminal record
- Driving records

The only information that is reflected on a credit report is how you repay a loan. Bounced checks, for example, do not become part of your credit file or your credit score. Bouncing a check will put your name in a national system so that others won't take your checks, but it will not affect your credit score.

How to Clean Up Your Credit Score

If you don't like what you see on your credit report, you can take steps to clean it up. First, sit down and highlight all the bad

GEEKOID

Here are some do's and don'ts for getting your credit report in good shape.

Do:

- Pay off as many loans as possible. A loan paid in full ups your credit score.
- Make all payments on time.
- Use only one or two credit cards, and cancel all others.
- Keep the oldest credit cards open and close the newest ones, unless the old one has a rate that is significantly higher (you can probably call and negotiate this down).
- Pay down balances on your credit cards.
- Pay down delinquent balances first.
- If you're trying to up your score, get a line of credit for something you have the cash for, and then pay it off in a short amount of time.
- Check your credit reports at least annually for accuracy.

Don't

- Open too many new credit cards or other lines of credit in a short amount of time.
- Close too many credit card accounts at once, especially older, more established lines of credit.
- Make late payments or miss payments.
- Max out your credit cards.
- Get more credit than you can repay as agreed.
- Not have credit—if you've never had credit, it's hard to get credit.

accounts on your credit report. If you still owe them money, call them and tell them you'll send the balance if they'll take the bad history off your credit report. Some companies will do this, even though it's not publicized.

If you've paid the entire balance, but had some late payments, call the company and tell them that you had some trouble, but still paid them in full. Ask them if they'll remove the bad history as a one-time courtesy to a valued customer. They often do this. If they say no, call back at a different time and ask a different person. You may get different results. In the end, it will be worth all the work to get even one or two slow payment histories removed.

 *Do not neglect to pay any money you owe to anyone. Even an item as small as an overdue library fine could end up on your credit report.*

After you've cleaned up your credit report as much as possible, start taking action to get your score up. Here are some tried-and-true ways to do that.

- Get a secured credit card. This is basically a credit card for which the bank has the money in reserve. You give the bank $1,000, and they issue a credit card with a $1,000 limit. They have their money, so they aren't risking anything. That's why it's called secured. You should use it each month, being sure never to go over your limit and to always pay the balance in full each month and pay it on time. After about a year, you can ask the bank to convert this into an unsecured account instead of secured. At this point, they return to you the $1,000 they were holding to secure the card.

GEEKOID

The Fair Debt Collection Practices Act says that a debt collector may not call you before 8:00 a.m., after 9:00 p.m., or at work if the collector knows that your employer disapproves of the calls. Collectors may not harass you, make false statements, or use unfair practices when trying to collect a debt. They must honor a written request from you to stop further contact.

• Get a loan with a cosigner, such as a parent or sibling. The cosigner is taking responsibility for the loan if you default, so this isn't something you want to ask of most friends, but it's a good way to repair credit or get credit when you're young. After about a year of paying the loan on time, you can ask the financial institution to refinance in your name only, which will help you even more on the road to better credit.

GEEKSpeak:

"No man's credit is ever as good as his money."

Ed Howe

• Get a cell phone and other credit that is easy to get. These include department store credit cards and loans from high-interest loan companies. It is sometimes worth it to get these higher-interest loans and pay them off quickly to raise your credit score.

As you are paying off debts you legitimately owe, you will also want to check for incorrect information that may be on your report. There

A **secured credit card** is one that has a set dollar limit, an amount that has already been put in reserve in the bank.

may be simple errors there, or perhaps there is information that applies to someone with a name similar or identical to yours.

To maintain accuracy once you have cleaned up your credit report, be sure and get a copy of your report at least once a year. This will allow you to stay on top of problems and correct them as soon as possible. Begin to build a good rating by starting with a secured credit card, or getting a loan with a co-signer.

Do not waste your time or money on credit repair agencies or credit counseling agencies. They cannot remove negative information from your credit report, and can only give you the advice I've given you here. They may do some of the leg work for you, but if your credit is bad, it's probably because you don't have a lot of extra money. You're better off doing this task for yourself and putting the money you save toward creating positive credit transactions.

GEEK AT A GLANCE

- A credit report can be a tool to help you get your financial affairs in order.

- Information in your credit history is gathered by credit bureaus that gather and make it available to potential creditors, insurance companies, and potential employers.

- Credit reports include a credit score, a three-digit number that is computed based on information in the report. The numbers range from 300 to 850, with the higher number indicating a better credit risk.

- Credit scores are used by potential lenders to determine if they'll lend you money. Prospective employers may also use them to learn information about you if you apply for a job.

- You are entitled to one free copy of your credit report per year. You may receive more for a small fee.

- You are also eligible for a free copy if you've been turned down for credit, or if you've been a victim of identity theft.

- Once you get your credit report, clean up items that indicate problems in your financial picture.

BLUEPRINT FOR A BUDGET

You will never be able to control your money and have it work for you unless you know exactly how much you have and where it's going.

You need some instrument to tell you exactly how much money you have coming in, and how much you are spending, and where. That's right. You need a budget.

Don't let the B word scare you. This isn't as bad as it sounds. Like losing weight or trying to stop smoking, setting a budget is something a lot of people set out to do, but can't stick to. But it is possible to develop a budget that takes into account your unique needs, and helps you make your money work for you.

The good news is that just setting a budget and reviewing it regularly is more than most people do, so if you're even considering doing it, you're way ahead of the game. Writing down income versus expenses is a good way to see how much extra money (if any) you have after paying your bills each month. If you start out in the negative on paper, then you know right away that something has to change. If you have lots of extra money, then you will get a feel for how much you should be saving.

GEEK Speak:

"I'm living so far beyond my income that we may almost be said to be living apart."
E.E. Cummings

How a Budget Should Look

Although each budget will be as individual as the person who created it, there are general guidelines for how much you should allow for items such as your home, car, and savings. These are percentages of after-tax income, so take taxes right off the top— they're usually fixed and can't be adjusted.

- 35% for housing – mortgage or rent, utilities, insurance, taxes, and home maintenance

- 20% for transportation – car payments, auto insurance, tag or license fees, maintenance, gasoline, and parking

GEEK Speak:

"A budget tells us what we can't afford, but it doesn't keep us from buying it."
William Feather

- 20% for other items – food, clothing, entertainment, child care, medical expenses, tithing, and charity

- 15% for debt – consumer debt, student loans, retail installment contracts, credit cards, personal loans, tax debts, and medical debts

- 10% for savings – a minimum throughout your working life. Once you get out of debt (excluding car and home payments), you should be saving up to 25%.

GEEK Speak:

"Why is there so much month left at the end of the money?"
John Barrymore

Your savings should never drop below 10%, and really should be more than that. The only time it's okay not to save is if you are on a short-term plan to reduce your debt significantly. But make sure this short-term arrangement doesn't become a long-term one.

Making Your Budget

First, let's see how your own finances stack up to these general guidelines. In the table below, fill in what you spend each month in each category. Start out with the things that are constant, such as rent or mortgage, car payment(s), insurance, and taxes, then move on to the items that vary. For the purpose of this exercise, write down what you spent in the flexible categories last month.

HOUSING (35%)

Mortgage ....$ _____
Rent ....$ _____
Utilities ....$ _____
Taxes ....$ _____
Insurance...$ _____
Maintenance (includes condo fees if applicable) ....$ _____
Other ....$ _____
Amount Spent ($) ....$ _____
Amount Spent (%) ....% _____

TRANSPORTATION (20%)

Car Payment .... $ _____
Auto Insurance .... $ _____
Tag or License .... $ _____
Maintenance .... $ _____
Gas .... $ _____
Parking .... $ _____
Other .... $ _____
Amount Spent ($) .... $ _____
Amount Spent (%) .... % _____

OTHER (20%)

Food .... $ _____
Clothing .... $ _____
Entertainment .... $ _____
Child Care .... $ _____
Pet Care .... $ _____
Medical Expenses .... $ _____
Tithing/Charity .... $ _____
Other .... $ _____
Amount Spent ($) .... $ _____
Amount Spent (%) .... % _____

DEBT (15%)

Student Loans .... $ _____
Credit Cards .... $ _____
Personal Loans .... $ _____
Other Debt .... $ _____
(insert home or car)
Amount Spent ($) .... $ _____
Amount Spent (%) .... % _____

SAVINGS (10%)

Savings Account ....$ _____
IRA ....$ _____
401(k) ....$ _____
Profit Sharing ....$ _____
Amount Spent ($) ....$ _____
Amount Spent (%) ....% _____

Every penny you spend should be written down. If you didn't keep up with every item last month, try tracking it this month. You'll be surprised how small expenses add up. Purchases you make instinctively, such as spending $1.50 a day on a soda that you could have brought from home for $.25 can cost almost $500 a year. How about money you spent on books you could've gotten from the library? Little things can make a big difference. And note that you should include what you spent on a credit card, not what you paid your credit card company. You may have spent $1,000 but paid only $200. We're looking for spending patterns, not payment patterns.

Now that you've completed each category, here is the moment of truth!

- Question number one: Did you spend more than you made?

- Question number two: Did you save any money?

GEEK*Speak:*

"I've got all the money I'll ever need, if I die by four o'clock."
Henny Youngman

GEEK*Speak:*

"Budget: A mathematical confirmation of your suspicions."
A.A. Latimer

Look at your numbers to help you answer these questions. If you spent more than you made, you need to change something. If you did not save any money, you need to change something. Is anything out of line? Do you make $20,000 a year and drive a $40,000 car? You should probably sell your car and get a new (old) one.

Of course, under special circumstances the amounts allotted will have to be revised. For example, if you, your spouse, or your child has special medical needs, then you will have to adjust your housing and transportation expenses to allow for the extra medical expenses. If you walk to work and don't need a car, you can take the money you won't need for transportation and put it in your housing or savings percentages (or any other category you choose).

Once you get the amounts adjusted to realistic amounts, you have your budget! That wasn't so hard was it?

Using general guidelines, you can create a budget tailored to your needs.

Living Within Your Means

Here's the part that's tougher. Now that you have your budget established, your job is to live within the limits you've set for yourself in each category. Start to take action to keep your spending in line with the entries. Stop spending more than you make, and you'll feel you're less stressed. There are many ways to cut spending without feeling too much pain. Some of those are listed below.

- Shop smart – Buy items in bulk at wholesale companies. And buy only what you need, steering clear of the impulse items they sell at the front of the store. Toilet paper, paper towels, condiments, sodas, water, laundry detergent, cleaning products, and other

GEEKOID

Look for clothes, shoes, accessories, linens, and bedding at discount stores like T.J. Maxx, Marshall's, Stein Mart, and Target instead of at the mall. They often have the same items for around half the price.

necessities are almost always priced much lower there than at the grocery store or quick mart. Plus you save time and gas by buying all items in one place and making trips less frequently. However, wine, electronics, and jewelry may not be such a good deal, especially if you make a purchase you hadn't planned on making.

- Lower your utility bills – Lower your heating and cooling bills by making sure your windows and doors seal properly, and by not keeping your home too warm in the winter or too cool in the summer. Wear more layers when it's cold out and keep small space heaters if you only need one room to be warm (like a bathroom!). Wear lighter clothes in the summer and drink lots of water to stay cool. Use a ceiling fan in your bedroom to make it feel cooler while you sleep.

GEEKOID

Lower your power bills by using electronics more effectively. Turn lights off when you leave rooms, don't leave TV sets on if you aren't watching them, don't leave your computer on when you're not using it, and don't use the dryer for items that you could hang dry. Don't use your regular oven when a toaster oven will do.

- Live conservatively – Don't live in a bigger home than you need. It doesn't make sense to heat, cool, maintain, furnish, and insure more home than you use. If you have that much extra money, save it for a rainy day or buy a vacation home.

GEEK Speak:

"Budgeting: A method of worrying before you spend instead of afterward."

Anonymous

- Drive smart – Don't drive or insure more car than you need. If you never or rarely have another passenger in your car, consider getting a smaller, less expensive, more fuel-efficient model. Newer, bigger, more expensive cars cost you more in payments, interest, gas, and insurance. Buying a car as a status symbol is not a geek-friendly move.

- Entertain yourself – Wait for movies to come out on DVD instead of going to the theater. It costs much less, is more convenient, and allows you to save on drinks and snacks. Look for free entertainment. This includes exercise, such as taking a walk, going hiking at a state park, and reading or watching TV instead of going to expensive restaurants and movies.

GEEKOID

Borrow books from the library instead of buying them new (excluding this one, naturally). Sometimes you can also find movies at your local library.

- Work more – If you're really bored, and none of the above entertainment options interest you, get a part-time job. It can be a great way to make new friends and fill your time making money, not spending it.

 **GEEK AT A GLANCE**

- You will never get control of your money unless you have a clear idea of how much is coming in, and how much is going out.

- The best way to gain control of your money is to develop a budget.

- Add up your monthly income (after taxes).

- Make a list of your monthly commitments.

- Adjust amounts as needed to allow for special needs and circumstances.

- Decide how much money you can save, and start planning to do so.

THE POWER AND PITFALLS OF PLASTIC

Most financial experts agree that the smart thing to do is have only one or two credit cards and always pay your balance in full.

While not carrying credit card debt is certainly the goal, one thing that a lot of financial advisors fail to mention is that using a credit card is using free money for the length of your billing cycle. So use them, but be sure you can pay off the balance when the bill comes in the mail. I use a credit card for almost everything I purchase, including groceries, gas, and clothing purchases, as well as at restaurants and movies—really anywhere that will take credit cards. And here's why:

GEEK Speak:

"My problem lies in reconciling my gross habits with my net income."

Errol Flynn

- Because it's free money for twenty to thirty days, as long as you pay your bill on time and in full.

- It makes it easier to budget and makes my life simpler. I write one check or make one online payment instead of writing several checks or having to keep up with debits daily.

- It makes record-keeping simpler. At tax time, I go through my credit card statements for the entire year and highlight deductible items. This makes it simple to track spending for medical expenses, office supplies, and other tax deductible expenses.

- And here's the best reason – I get rebates on everything I purchase. I use a credit card issued by a gas company, and I get a 5 percent rebate on gasoline purchases and a 1 percent rebate on everything else. Between business and personal expenses, my husband and I spend an average of $5,000 per month that we put on a credit card, so I get about $40 a month in free gas credits. That's a great deal.

Using credit cards can offer advantages such as not having to pay for purchases immediately, and rebates based on purchases. Just be sure to pay your balance in full each month so you do not build up debt.

How to Choose a Credit Card

No doubt you'll get lots of credit card offers in the mail. But you should be selective in choosing which one to accept, or if you don't get an offer, which one(s) to apply for. The most important thing is to know the details of what you'll be getting. Here are some things to look out for as you shop around.

If you expect to pay your bill in full each month, shop for a card that has no annual fee, and a longer grace period (the time between the purchase and when you actually have to pay).

If you sometimes carry over a balance to the next month, a lower interest rate would be helpful.

If you expect to use your card to get cash advances, look for a card that

GEEK GLOSSARY

The interest charged on a credit card is referred to as the **annual percentage rate**, or **APR**.

GEEKOID

Grace periods usually only apply to new purchases. Most cards do not offer a grace period for cash advances and balance transfers. Also, if you carry over a part of your balance from a preceding month, you may not have a grace period for even new purchases.

offers a lower APR and lower fees on cash advances. Be aware that some cards charge a higher APR for cash advances than for purchases.

Check to see if there is a minimum finance charge, or if actual charges will apply if they are less.

GUERRILLA GEEK

Check carefully into the APRs of a credit card before you apply for it. A single credit card may have several APRs, which might include these variations:

- One for purchases, another for cash advances, and another for balance transfers
- Different rates for different balances
- A penalty APR for late payments
- An introductory APR that is offered for a limited time
- A delayed APR

Here are some other fees that some card companies charge. You'll want to know about these ahead of time so your card doesn't end up costing you more than it's worth.

GEEK*Speak:*

"Money talks—but credit has an echo."
Bob Thaves

- Annual fee – charged for having the card; these are sometimes charged monthly.

- Cash advance fee – charged when you use the card for a cash advance; this may be a flat fee, or may be a percentage of the advance.

- Balance-transfer fee – charged when you transfer a balance from another card. This may be done with "checks" provided to pay off another card. This is usually 3 percent.

- Late-payment fee – charged if your payment is received after the due date. These can sometimes be substantial.

- Over-the-credit-limit fee – charged if you go over your credit limit.

GEEK GLOSSARY

Revolving credit: An agreement by a bank or other financial institution to lend a specific amount to a borrower, and to allow that amount to be borrowed again once it has been repaid. Credit cards are usually considered revolving credit.

- Set-up fee – charged when a new credit card is opened.

- Return-item fee – charged if you pay your bill by check and the check bounces.

GEEK Speak:

"Money often costs too much."
Ralph Waldo Emerson

- Other fees – some card companies charge a fee if you pay by telephone transfer, and for other services such as reporting to credit bureaus and other customer services.

Know what incentives and other features are offered. Here are some you might encounter.

- Rebates – money back on your purchases

- Frequent flier miles – miles are given in relation to the amount spent

- Supplemental warranties – additional coverage for purchases

According to *Forbes Magazine*, Bill Gates has enough money to buy lunch for every person on Earth.

- Insurance – car rental insurance or travel accident insurance

- Card registration – a record of your account numbers to be reported if your wallet is stolen or lost

GEEKOID

Some credit cards may also offer, for a price, insurance to cover your card balance if you become unemployed, disabled, or die, and insurance to cover the first $50 of charges if someone steals and uses your card. By law you are not responsible for charges over that $50.

How to Use a Credit Card to Your Advantage

If you decide to use a credit card for any or all of the reasons I mentioned above, here are some practical ways you can get it to work the most for you.

- Choose a card with a rebate you can easily use. I've tried cards that earn free airline mileage, free gifts from catalogs, and various other rebates that require spending money to get something for free. I'd rather be able to choose the best rate when I fly, rather than dealing with trading in mileage for limited flights with blackout dates. Many cards out there offer rebates on everyday items such as gas and groceries. That way you don't have to spend money to get your rebate.

GEEK*Speak:*

"A pig bought on credit is forever grunting."
Spanish Proverb

- Don't have too many credit cards—it's simply too hard to pay them all in full and on time. Making a late payment because you forget or just don't have time is costly, and easily avoided. If you open a new credit card to save 10 or 20 percent on a large purchase, pay it off and close it right away. By right away I mean as soon as you're going to start accruing interest.

Some department stores offer six months interest free. Definitely take advantage of that. But don't wait until the end of the six months. Either make equal payments each month so that it's paid off before interest starts accruing, or put away enough money each month in a savings account to pay off the amount at the end. But be careful—with most of these offers, if you don't pay the balance off before the expiration date of the no-

GUERRILLA GEEK

The first credit card was issued by Diners Club in the early 1950s. The purpose was to spare users from carrying large sums of cash when dining out.

GUERRILLA GEEK

There's more than one good reason not to carry a lot of credit cards. The obvious reason is that the fewer you carry, the less tempted you are to overuse them. But also, if you have too many open accounts, even if you have zero balances, potential creditors view this as risky because you have the ability to run up a lot of credit quickly, whether you intend to or not.

interest offer, interest will be computed retroactively on the entire amount.

Just as important as knowing what you can expect a credit card to do for you, there are some things you should never do when using them. You should *never*:

• Make late payments.

• Carry a balance.

• Take advantage of the checks credit card companies send (they usually carry a 1 percent fee for transferring balances, and the balance starts to accrue interest immediately).

• Pay an annual fee, unless your rebates greatly exceed that fee.

If You Have Credit Card Debt

Despite the best of intentions, we all know that credit card debt happens. But when it does, use these tips to get the debt paid down as quickly as possible.

• Make payments on time. The late fees can be astronomical, and after one or more late payments, most credit cards raise your interest rate. So in addition to the $35 late fee, your interest could go up to as high as 24 percent—it could double or triple after just a few late payments.

• Try not to use cards with a balance for new purchases. Some credit card companies apply any amount you pay to the older debt, meaning even if you pay your new charges plus a certain amount toward your carried debt, they may charge you interest on the entire amount. Most people don't have the patience or time to figure out how it's calculated. My advice is to have one card for monthly charges that you pay in full, and another that is carrying debt. Know how much you can pay toward the latter card each month to get it paid off in a reasonable amount of time.

GEEK*Speak:*

"The only reason a great many American families don't own an elephant is that they have never been offered an elephant for a dollar down and easy weekly payments."
Mad Magazine

GUERRILLA GEEK

One way to help control your credit card spending each month is to get a charge card instead of a credit card. American Express, for example, is a charge card, meaning you are required to pay your balance in full each month. They do have an annual fee, but spending $35 a year to help you stay in control could save you well more than that in interest.

A **charge card** is a card that simply lets you charge your purchases, but does not extend credit, meaning the balance must be paid in full each month. A **credit card** is issued by a company extending credit, meaning you can make payments on your debt on an agreed-upon basis.

- After a period of paying all your bills on time, call and ask for a rate reduction. If the card company won't lower your rate, shop for a lower rate on a new card and transfer the balance. Always read the fine print and know what the balance transfer fee is (usually 1 to 3 percent), what the annual fee is, and the length of time you will get the introductory rate. Use spreadsheet software to make sure you're really getting a better deal.

- The only way to pay down debt on a credit card is to pay a large percentage of the balance every month. If you don't have enough extra money to do this, you should get a second job or cut back on other expenses. Otherwise you'll never get out of debt. One year of a part-time job will do a lot toward reducing your debt and securing your future.

Getting a Credit Card if Your Credit is Bad

Naturally, you will not want to get a credit card to go further into debt if you already owe money, or if you have a bad credit history. But if you're starting to clean up your act, and need a place to get a foothold to begin to do better, here are some ways you might be able to get a credit card to start over.

- Apply for a credit card at a small, locally owned store. Sometimes people who know you are more willing to give you a chance.

- Check with the bank or credit union where you already have an account. Since you're already a customer, they may be willing to give you a credit card.

- Apply for a secured credit card, one for which you'll be required to open an account as security. Your credit line will be a percentage of your deposit.

- Ask a friend or family member to co-sign with you for a card. Be sure to choose someone who has good credit of his or her own. Be sure you can be responsible about the account,

GEEKOID

Here's a tip for not getting hurt by security measures taken by your credit card company: Call before you are about to do anything out of the ordinary. Without advance notice, the company may decline the charge. For example, if you're planning to travel to another country, or if you're about to make a large purchase, give your card company a call first to smooth the way.

GEEK GLOSSARY

Credit limit is the maximum you will be allowed to charge to your card. If you exceed that amount, you may be charged an over-the-credit-limit fee.

though, because if you default, it will taint your friend's record as well as yours.

• Don't overspend once you get a card. Only buy things for which you have the money in hand, then pay them off as soon as the bill comes.

GUERRILLA GEEK

The term credit card was first used in 1887 by lawyer and author Edward Bellamy, but his idea of how it should be used is very different from what we know today. He dreamed of a society in which each citizen would be given a yearly card, issued by the government, which would pay for all goods and services throughout the year. The dollar amount of each card would be the citizen's "share of the annual product of the nation." When purchases were made, the card would be punched according to the value of the item.

GEEK AT A GLANCE

- As long as you are careful not to overuse them, credit cards can be a useful financial tool.

- Credit cards can offer you a grace period before you actually have to pay for purchases, and they can offer incentives like rebates, to help you actually earn money.

- Be careful to investigate cards carefully before you apply for them.

- There are several features you should know about the cards you get, such as all fees involved, and if full or partial payments are expected each month.

- If you find you are racking up too much credit card debt, switch to a charge card that requires you to pay your entire balance each month.

- Use your cards wisely to have them work for you.

CHECKLIST FOR CHECKING ACCOUNTS

A checking account is one of the most important tools you need, but is also the most basic. Almost everyone needs one, and it should be one that doesn't cost anything.

There are just a few options to consider as you get ready to open an account. Shop around to find the best checking account for your purposes, and use it wisely.

Identifying the Best Account for You

Before you go to the bank to open your checking account, think carefully about some of the options you'll have. You can compare options online for most banks. Here are some common types of checking accounts, and the things you'll be offered.

- Basic account – This is for the customer who uses a checking account for little more than just paying bills. You will not earn interest in this account. Some of these basic accounts require direct deposit, and a low minimum balance to avoid fees. Most of the time, however, these accounts are free of charge, except for the cost of the checks you order, and sometimes those are free as well. Here are some common benefits of these accounts.

GEEKOID

Online Banking Myths

Many people think it's unsafe to bank online. To the contrary, experts say that if you rely on paper you are much more likely to have your identity stolen. According to a recent study, the average paper-based identity fraud nets more than $4,500 per incident. The average online incident is just over $500. Getting paper statements makes it far too easy for thieves to get your info. And shredding doesn't provide as much protection as you think – most thieves just take the paper from your mailbox before it ever gets to you. That is far easier than going through your garbage.

- No monthly or yearly service charge
- No annual fee for ATM/debit cards
- No fee for ATM withdrawals from your bank
- No fee for ATM withdrawals from other banks. It's a rare perk, but some banks do offer it. Particularly if you travel a lot, or often find yourself far from your local branch, this is a big one.
- Free checks
- No limit on the number of checks you can write

- Interest bearing account – The only reason you should ever have an interest-bearing checking account is if you float lots of money every month,

GEEK*Speak:*

"I am opposed to millionaires, but it would be dangerous to offer me the position."
Mark Twain

and the amounts are large enough that the interest earned would outweigh the fees for these accounts.

GUERRILLA GEEK

When investigating account options, ask for a complete list of all fees involved. Some banks now require a small fee for free checking if you don't use direct deposit.

Most interest-bearing checking accounts don't give you anything for free. You have to pay for checks, ATM/debit cards, and monthly service charges. Make sure the interest earned, usually paid monthly, surpasses these fees. If you have a large income and it would behoove you to earn interest while waiting to pay your bills, or if you are quickly reimbursed for business expenses and have a grace period before paying your credit card bill, an interest-bearing checking   account may be the best option for you.

However, the goal is to use checking accounts simply to pay bills—any money that you're not using should be in a savings or investment account, where it earns a lot more money.

Shop around to find a checking account that doesn't cost anything.

- Express accounts – These are designed for people who prefer to bank by ATM, telephone, or personal computer. They usually offer unlimited check writing, require low minimum balances, and low or no monthly fees. The downside? There are teller fees for each visit to the bank, or a flat monthly fee to cover the visits. Check with your bank for specifics.

- Premium accounts – These accounts offer extra features such as free travelers' checks, free money orders, cashier checks, and may even offer a small accidental death insurance policy. These services will have a small monthly service fee, but can be worth the expense if you use them often.

When more than one person has use of an account, accurate management is critical. Each person needs to carefully record any checks written, or withdrawals made.

- Senior/student checking – These accounts accommodate the special needs of those just starting out and those possibly entering retirement. The benefits of these accounts will vary according, to particular banks, but may include no-fee checks, cashier's and traveler's checks, ATM use, plus better rates on loans and credit cards.

GUERRILLA GEEK

Advantages of Online Banking

- Saves time and money – no check writing, no postage, no waiting in lines
- Your payments get posted faster – most online payments get processed within one day
- Saves space – no more filing all those paper statements

GEEKOID

Once you've chosen the type of account you want, you'll need to identify the bank that will best meet your needs. Choose one that's convenient to home and/or work, and one that offers extras you might need, like being open on Saturday. Some banks even offer help with disabilities, such as special communication equipment to help customers who are deaf. Don't just find out what you'll get up front for opening an account—find out what services you'll receive on a day-to-day basis.

• Money market – This account combines checking with savings and/or investment features for those who want to pay bills, but also earn interest as well. It requires a high minimum deposit to open—usually $1,000 to $10,000—and the number of checks that can be written per statement period is limited.

How to Use Your Checking Account

Your checking account will probably be the account that you have to monitor most often. You should keep a close watch on your balance, keeping track of every check you write, every ATM withdrawal, and every transaction using your debit card.

There are several methods to keep track of your account, from the simple hand-written log to software both straightforward (Excel, Lotus, etc.) and more complex (Quicken, Microsoft Money). If you're in the dark about technology, keep a written record. If you have a computer but don't want or need anything complex, an Excel spreadsheet does the math for you without a lot of fuss.

If you own your own business, have complex finances, or just like gadgets, you may want to go try Quicken or other programs like it. Unless you have lots of time and are good with software, my recommendation is to keep it simple and go with the Excel option.

 *The most important rule of checking accounts? Don't bounce checks.*

No matter what account works best for you, and what method you choose for keeping up with expenses paid from your account, you must keep accurate records so you will not spend more money than you have in your account. Besides being diligent in your record keeping, here are some other ways to keep from bouncing checks.

GEEKOID

Don't forget to enter automatic payments into your check register. Because they're made without your input each month, they may easily drop off the financial radar, which can be a costly mistake.

- Buffer funds. Keep a certain amount in your account that you ignore. I know people who have $500 or $1,000 in their account that they never include in their balance. That just-in-case cash can save you a lot of money—and headaches.

- Overdraft protection. There are two types. The first is a line of credit that loans you money automatically if your checking

GEEK*Speak:*

"We can tell our values by looking at our checkbook stubs."
Gloria Steinem

account balance goes below zero. Most banks charge a flat fee for each transfer, in addition to interest that starts accruing immediately. The second type links your savings account to your checking account so money is automatically transferred if you're overdrawn. There are usually fees for this type of transfer as well, but they are nominal compared to the fees you'll accrue if you bounce a check without overdraft protection.

GEEK*Speak:*

"Money can't buy you happiness, but it does bring you a more pleasant form of misery."

Spike Milligan

- Eagle eyes. At the very least, always balance your checking account each month when you receive your statement in the mail. I also check my account online at least once a week, reconciling my record of activity with the bank's. It's a good way for me to keep up with cash withdrawals and debit card use by my spouse and daughter.

Checking Account Tracking Systems

Unfortunately, you aren't the only one that will know if you bounce a check, or two. Just like the credit bureaus that report your habits on paying your bills, there are systems that record your checking account habits. If you bounce checks even on an occasional basis, retailers who subscribe to check-tracking services may not take your checks. And even worse, if you are a habitual check bouncer, your bank can close your account. Having that noted in the database may make it hard (or even impossible) to get another bank to open an account. Events are kept on file for five years.

GEEKOID

Bouncing a check can cost you a lot. Most bank charges for insufficient funds are now around the $40 mark, and the person to whom you wrote the check may charge you another $40. When they assess this charge, you may have another check bounce, and it becomes a vicious cycle that's hard to escape. Keep an eye on that bottom line!

Under the Fair and Accurate Credit Transaction Act (FACTA) amendments to the Fair Credit Reporting Act (FCRA), you are entitled to a free copy of your debit report, at your request, once every twelve months.

GEEK GLOSSARY

A **debit history** contains facts about you and your deposit or checking account history. It is made available by law to your current and prospective financial institutions to indicate the likelihood of your managing your debit accounts responsibly. It can include the following:

- Checking account closures you have had
- Number and frequency of bounced checks
- Number and dates of inquiries about your accounts
- Number and frequency of check orders

GEEK🔍OID

The following information will not be included in your debit history.

- Race
- Personal lifestyle
- Medical history
- Religious preference
- Political preference
- Criminal record

To request a free copy of your ChexSystems report, go to:

www.consumerdebit.com/consumerinfo/us/en/chexsystems/report/index.html

To Order by Phone
Call (800) 428-9623

GUERRILLA GEEK

Never make a debit card purchase without having funds to cover it. If you make a debit card (POS) purchase, the computer looks to see if you have the funds. If you don't, the transaction may go through anyway, plus a $35-40 fee. Even if you deposit the money the next morning before the transaction clears, you'll be charged a fee for having insufficient funds (NSF).

POS is an abbreviation for point of sale or point of service. It can mean a retail store where a transaction takes place or may refer to the electronic cash register system used there. **NSF** means non-sufficient funds, or that a demand for payment cannot be honored because there is not enough money in a particular account.

To order a ChexSystems report by mail:
> Print the complete order form at the web site, and mail to
> ChexSystems
> Attn: Consumer Relations
> 7805 Hudson Road, Suite 100
> Woodbury, MN 55125

To order by fax:
> Print and complete order form at the web site
> Fax to Consumer Relations at (602) 659-2197

To request a free copy of your SCAN report, go to:

www.consumerdebit.com/consumerinfo/us/en/scan/report/index.html

To Order by Phone:
> Call (800) 262-7771. Be prepared to provide the phone operator with your name, address, driver's license number, and checking account number.

GEEKOID

By law, your debit report can only be disclosed to others having a legitimate right to that information. Such requests would include:

- In response to your own written instruction
- In compliance with a court order or federal grand jury subpoena
- For employment purposes
- In the course of a business transaction
- If required for a child support determination

Anyone who willfully and knowingly obtains a debit history under false pretenses may be fined and imprisoned.

To Order by Mail:
> Print and complete an order form from the website and mail to:
> Deposit Payment Protection Services, Inc.
> Attn: Consumer Referral Services
> 7805 Hudson Road, Suite 100
> Woodbury, MN 55125

To Order by fax:
> Print and complete an order form and fax to
> Deposit Payment Protection Services, Inc. at (800) 358-4506

GUERRILLA GEEK

You've probably received notification from your bank about Check 21. If you ignored it, it could cost you money. Check 21, short for the Check Clearing for the 21st Century Act, went into effect October 28, 2004. It is a system whereby companies can turn your paper check into an electronic image and speed the image and data through the system. What does it mean? It means that checks can clear as quickly as ATM or debit card transactions, instead of taking seven to ten days to clear. Never write a check without having the money in your account to cover it! Don't count on "float" time—it may no longer be there.

GEEK AT A GLANCE

- Almost everyone needs a checking account as a way to pay bills.

- Several different types of accounts exist. Research and learn what each one offers so you'll know which is best for you.

- Monitor your account carefully so you do not bounce checks.

- Account activity is often monitored by debit reporting companies that collect that information and report it when requested.

THE NECESSITY OF NEST EGGS

If you've made it through the first few chapters, you should be out of debt, living on a budget, and able to save and invest lots of money each month. Excellent. So now what? What is the simplest, best plan for saving?

The answer is the same as for other areas of personal finance: the one that you have time to manage. If it's not easy to do, you're probably not going to do it.

Options for Saving

For most people, that means automatic payroll deductions that are tied to a savings account. Set up a system that deducts automatically, and that you only have to check on once or twice a year. For the purpose of this chapter, I am referring to regular, short-term savings, meaning money you have instant access to, as opposed to retirement and long-term savings, which I'll address in a later chapter.

GEEK*Speak:*

"A bank book makes good reading—better than some novels."
Harry Lauder

Most savings accounts don't accrue a lot of interest, but you'll earn some, and will have cash for emergencies. There are other factors besides just the interest, though. Here are some ways you can save and some things you should consider.

APR (Annual Percentage Rate) is the percentage of interest to be paid on funds in your account. Simply, if the APR is 10 percent, and you have $100, the interest would be $10. APY (Annual Percentage Yield) is the percentage of interest to be earned based on an institution's compounding method, assuming funds remain in the account for a 365-day year. If the APR is 10 percent on $100, and interest is compounded monthly, you'd earn $10 the first month, giving you $110. Then the next month, your interest would be calculated on $110. This would continue each month.

All banks and credit unions tell you the APR and APY, making it easier to compare savings rates. The key items to ask is how often interest is compounded.

- Interest-bearing checking accounts – This is just what its name implies: a checking account that earns interest. It's the lowest-paying type of account, but also the easiest for keeping cash flowing. You can keep all of your money in an interest-bearing checking account, including the money you use to live on each month. You'll usually earn a small amount of interest and pay a monthly fee. You're usually better off using a free, no-interest checking account for fast-moving money, and putting the rest in another savings vehicle, but it depends on what fees your bank charges and your average daily balance.

- Regular savings – These accounts hold money you don't plan to dip into very often. They earn a little more money than interest-bearing checking accounts, but usually not as much as money markets or CDs. Savings accounts usually have low minimum balances, low monthly fees, and few restrictions on the number of withdrawals or transfers you can make.

GEEKOID

Two characteristics of a savings account are that 1) the funds are liquid (meaning they can easily be cashed in with no loss of principal), and 2) they are insured against losses.

Savings accounts are good places for small amounts of money you don't plan to use often, but think you may need within the next six months. Savings accounts are usually FDIC insured for up to $100,000.

• Money market accounts (MMAs) – Money market accounts are really nothing more than high-interest savings accounts. They pay higher interest than regular savings accounts because they have high minimum balances, usually $5,000 to $10,000. They are called money market accounts because the interest rate is tied to the overall money market. It's a good place to put money you may need soon, but want to earn more interest on in the meantime.

GEEK*Speak:*

"The safe way to double your money is to fold it over once and put it in your pocket."

Frank Hubbard

Money market savings accounts usually limit the number of withdrawals and transfers you can make monthly—most limit you to no more than three checks a month. Deposits are

GEEK GLOSSARY

Simple interest is calculated by multiplying the principal times the rate of interest by the amount of time in years. **Compounding interest** is calculated on the principal plus the accumulated interest. The interest compounds because you're earning interest on interest.

unlimited, of course. Most money market accounts are FDIC insured up to $100,000.

• Certificates of Deposit (CDs) – CDs, also known as time deposits, or TDs, are great for money you don't plan to need within the next six to thirty-six months. Even though you purchase certificates, you don't need an actual piece of paper. Your balance will show up on a regular statement, just like a savings account. The earnings on a CD account are guaranteed at an agreed-upon rate at the time you open the account. In other words, they have a fixed interest rate and a fixed term.

GEEK Speak:

"A penny saved is a penny earned."
Ben Franklin

If you buy a twenty-four-month CD at 5 percent, you can't touch the money for two years, and the bank will pay you 5 percent a year on your balance. The interest is usually paid at maturity, meaning, in this case, at the end of the twenty-four-month period. A lot of people then keep the interest and buy another CD with the original amount, but you can also use all of the money to buy a new CD.

The bank can afford to pay more interest on CDs because you are telling them up front how long they will have your money. The bank can then use your funds to make loans to others, meaning they can use it to make money. But don't stress too much about putting your money here if there is a small possibility you'll need it sooner. You can always withdraw it sooner than agreed upon. You'll have to pay a

GUERRILLA GEEK

Some people think they're saving money by using the old money jar routine—they put their extra change in a jar at the end of every day, and then take the jar to the bank for deposit when it's full. That sounds like a novel idea, but in reality, it may cost you money. Some banks, and some grocery stories, where coins are sometimes traded for paper money, charge a fee for this service. It's taken on a "vending machine" quality, too, with the advent of machines that offer this service, and charge you a 10 percent fee. If you'd like to continue this practice and not lose money, consider these options:

- Exchange or deposit them at a bank that doesn't charge a fee.
- Use the coins for everyday expenses like postage stamps. You'll get 100 percent of the value of the coins this way.
- Instead of coins, save $1 bills.

penalty, but it's generally a chance worth taking to ensure a higher interest rate.

So what's the catch? Well, there's that pesky penalty for early withdrawal. Also, you're tying up money that could be otherwise invested. For example, you may get a thirty-six-month CD at 5 percent interest and find out the next month that your bank is offering thirty-six-month CDs for 6 percent. You can't just move your money to the higher-yielding CD on a whim. If you see much higher rates before your CD matures, you can weigh the penalty against higher earnings and see what will produce the most money in the long run.

GEEK*Speak:*

"A bank is a place that will lend you money if you can prove that you don't need it."

Bob Hope

Here's a quick summary of what's available.

INTEREST-BEARING CHECKING	CHECKING	SAVINGS	MONEY MARKET ACCOUNT	CDs
Interest	Low	Low	Good	Better
Minimum Balance	$100–$500	None	$5,000–$10,000	$5,000 and up
Account Fees	Low	Low	Low	Low
FDIC Insurance Limit	$100,000	$100,000	$100,000	$100,000
Minimum Length of Deposit	None	None	None	six months to three years
Maximum checks or withdrawals per month	None	None	3–10	N/A

Some banks offer flexible, or option, CDs. These usually offer one or more opportunities to add to your balance or withdraw from the balance, and also the opportunity to "bump up" your rate if the bank is offering a higher one. Check with your bank for details on all of its CD options. CDs are usually FDIC insured up to $100,000.

Here's my bottom-line advice. Keep your money to pay bills in a no-frills checking account, put six months' worth of savings in a regular savings or money market account, and put the rest in CDs. Remember the difference between savings and investments: savings are safer and more liquid than investments. True investments, such as mutual funds, stocks, or bonds are usually better vehicles for long-term savings, such as retirement accounts.

How Much to Save

It is really important to have a savings account, but how much you put in savings versus investments depends on considerations such as how dependable your job is, how much debt you have, what other safety nets you have (could you move in with family if you lost your house or job?), and whether you're averse to risk. You should set aside at least 10 percent of your income for

GEEK*Speak:*

"It's good to have money and the things that money can buy, but it's good, too, to check up once in a while and make sure that you haven't lost the things that money can't buy."

George Horace Lorimer

GEEK GLOSSARY

Federal Deposit Insurance Corporation (FDIC): an agency of the U.S. government that manages the bank-insurance funds, which insure deposits at banks and other qualifying financial institutions up to $100,000, per account, in interest and principal. FDIC insurance is mandatory for all nationally chartered banks and all banks that are members of the Federal Reserve System. The National Credit Union Association (NCUA) is its counterpart for credit unions.

all savings, including pure savings, investments, and retirement.

While you'll have to figure out your own safety zone between savings and investments, a good rule of thumb is that you should keep enough in savings to live on for at least six months, and put the rest in investments earning more interest. If you're young, in good health, have good, marketable job skills, and don't have a lot of debt, you should invest a lot more than you put in savings.

GEEKOID

A good way to save without feeling the pinch is to take any raise you get and immediately start putting it into your savings before you get used to the extra income.

GEEK AT A GLANCE

- There are many options for saving money. The simplest is to have it taken from your payroll check and deposited directly into a savings account.

- Before opening a savings account, evaluate your needs and match them to various savings methods. Here are some options to consider:

  - Interest-bearing checking account

  - Regular savings account

  - Money market accounts (MMAs)

  - Certificates of Deposit (CDs)

- How much you should save depends on a variety of factors such as the amount of debt you have, and how dependable your income is. In general, you should save about 10 percent of your income.

SUPPORTING YOUR UNCLE SAM

The subject of taxes is so broad that we can only touch briefly on it within this chapter. But perhaps we can at least answer some of the whys and whats of the topic.

Let's approach it this way: there are two main distinctions on how you pay taxes on what you earn. If you are employed, you pay your taxes by deductions from your paycheck. If you are self-employed, then you have to pay your taxes yourself directly to the IRS. While there's not much you can do about taxes, except through your vote, we can at least look and see what kind of money you're paying.

GEEK*Speak:*

"Taxation with representation ain't so hot either."
Gerald Barzan

GEEKOID

National Payroll Week celebrates America's 156 million wage earners and the payroll professionals that issue their paychecks. As the celebration's website indicates, "through the payroll withholding system, they contribute, collect, report and deposit approximately $1.4 trillion, or 71 percent, of the annual revenue of the U.S. Treasury." Singer/songwriter Brandon Sandefur's "America Works" has become the theme song of the week. Go to www.nationalpayrollweek.com for more info.

Taxes for the Employed

Who of us has not received a paycheck and been shocked at how little was left once deductions were made? Did you ever wonder just where all that money went? Here's a breakdown of the taxes taken out before you ever get to hold your check.

- Federal income taxes – Based on information that you provided when you started to work, your company will deduct money from each paycheck to go for federal income taxes. These go to the federal government to help pay for its services.

GEEKOID

On your first day of work, you'll complete the Form W-4, Employee's Withholding Allowance Certificate. This form helps your employer figure out how much federal income tax to take out of each paycheck. The more allowances (dependants) you claim, the less taxes you'll have taken out.

At the end of the year, when you file your income tax with the IRS, you'll compute the total amount of taxes you owe based on your entire year's income. If you have overpaid by way of deductions from your paychecks, you will file for a refund by April 15 of the following year. If you have underpaid, you will send the money in with your income tax form by that same date.

GEEK Speak:

"Taxes are what we pay for a civilized society."
U.S. Supreme Court Justice Oliver Wendell Holmes Jr.

GUERRILLA GEEK

You can check the latest tax rates by going to www.irs.gov, or by calling the IRS and requesting a tax table—I recommend the website!

- State and local taxes – Most states, and some cities, get a piece of your paycheck, and each one has different rules for how much they get.

- Social Security and Medicare – Both are completely supported by taxes from American workers. Social Security provides retirement income based on income during working years. Medicare offers health-care assistance to the elderly and disabled.

   You will no doubt see these listed on your paycheck under the heading of FICA. Social Security benefits include old-age, survivors, and disability insurance or OASDI. Medicare is the hospital insurance portion.

GEEKOID

You may also have voluntary deductions taken from your paycheck, such as for health insurance, or a 401(k) plan. You may even put aside money for child care or medical expenses not covered by insurance. Those dollars can be set aside before any taxes are taken out, which adds to the value of the savings.

GEEK GLOSSARY

Federal Insurance Contributions Act (FICA) tax is a United States employment tax levied in an equal amount on employees and employers to fund federal programs for retirees, the disabled, and children of deceased workers. The FICA taxes support Social Security and Medicare.

Your employer will deduct 6.2 percent of each of your paychecks for Social Security and 1.45 percent for Medicare, or $7.65 for every $100 you earn. But that's not all. You may be interested to know that your company is also paying, out of its own pocket, an equal amount on your behalf. The good news is that Social Security taxes only apply to your first $90,000 of income each year.

Although there may not be much you can do about taxes in general, there are some things you can do to cut the amount you have to pay, and to increase your savings.

GUERRILLA GEEK

Americans pay many taxes, including federal income tax, state and local income taxes, sales tax, and other taxes on specific items such as gasoline, cigarettes, and alcohol. The average American pays more than 50 percent of their income in combined taxes.

- Adjust your withholding – Check the paperwork you completed when you started to work. See how many allowances you claimed, and see if any of the information should be updated. More allowances, less money withheld.

- Make pre-tax contributions – Take advantage of employer-sponsored programs that allow you to contribute pre-tax money toward routine expenses such as health care, childcare, or retirement savings. Making these contributions up front reduces the amounts on which your taxes are computed. Examples would be 401(k) accounts, health-care flexible spending accounts, and flex accounts for dependent care.

GEEKOID

Make sure you understand how your taxes are calculated, and any deductions you may have. Talk to a tax advisor or financial advisor about ways to lower your tax liability. Remember, every tax dollar you save can be put toward your home or retirement, in turn saving you even more tax dollars!

GEEKOID

Ask your payroll department to help you decide how much money should be designated for your flex accounts, since you forfeit money left in the account at the end of the year. Also, check to be sure when you can sign up—it will probably be when you're first awarded benefits, or once per year during your employer's open enrollment period.

Taxes for the Self-employed

Even if you work for yourself, you still have to pay taxes. The difference is that instead of having an employer report your earnings and send taxes to the IRS for you, you'll have to do it yourself.

You know if you work for yourself, but the official definition from the Social Security website (www.ssa.gov/pubs/10022.html) is that "you are self-employed if you operate a trade, business or profession, either by yourself or as a partner." If you fit that definition, and if your net earnings are $400 or more in a year, you must report your earnings on Schedule SE (Form 1040) in addition to the other tax forms you must file. Here are some things you'll need to know:

GEEKOID

You can deduct half of your SE tax in figuring your adjusted gross income. Wage earners cannot deduct Social Security and Medicare taxes.

- SE tax rate – The self-employment tax rate is 15.3 percent. The rate consists of two parts: 12.4 percent for social security (old-age, survivors, and disability insurance) and 2.9 percent for Medicare (hospital insurance).

GEEK*Speak:*

"I'm proud to pay taxes in the United States; the only thing is, I could be just as proud for half the money."
Arthur Godfrey

- Maximum earnings subject to SE tax – Only the first $94,200 of your combined wages, tips, and net earnings in 2006 is subject to any combination of the 12.4 percent social security part of SE tax, Social Security tax, or railroad retirement tax.

GUERRILLA GEEK

If you're trying to compare employment (or self-employment) options, I suggest buying a tax computing program, like TurboTax. Save two different files, and key in the numbers. This is the quickest and most accurate way to compare $40,000 being employed to $40,000 being self-employed. You'll be able to see right away how any move you make will affect your total tax liability.

All your combined wages, tips, and net earnings in 2006 are subject to any combination of the 2.9 percent Medicare part of SE tax, social security tax, or railroad retirement tax.

- Self-employment tax deduction – You can deduct half of your SE tax in figuring your adjusted gross income. This deduction affects only your income tax. It does not affect either your net earnings from self-employment or your SE tax.

PAYING YOUR SELF-EMPLOYMENT TAXES

Estimated tax is how you will pay tax on self-employed income. In addition, this includes income from interest, dividends, alimony, rent, gains from the sale of assets, and prizes and awards. You may

If you have to pay estimated tax because your employer is not taking out enough, ask that more be taken out of your earnings.

also have to pay estimated tax if the amount of income tax being withheld from salary, pension, or other income is not enough.

Figure your estimated tax by figuring your expected adjusted gross income, taxable income, taxes, deductions, and credits for the year. It may be helpful to use your figures for the previous year as a guide.

Pay your taxes in quarterly installments. With regard to estimated tax, the year is divided into four payment periods. Each period has a specified due date. If you do not pay enough by the due date, you may be charged a penalty even if you are due a refund when you file your income tax. Payment period and due dates are shown below.

GEEK Speak:

"The taxpayer—that's someone who works for the federal government but doesn't have to take the civil service examination."

Ronald Reagan

For the period	Due date
Jan. 1 – March 31	April 15
April 1 – May 31	June 15
June 1 – August 31	September 15
September 1 – December 31	January 15 of next year

GEEKOID

For each self-employment tax period, the payments are due by the 15th, or the next business day if the 15th is on a Saturday or Sunday.

Go to the IRS website at www.irs.gov for more information. Click on Businesses, and click again on Small Business/Self-Employed. You'll be able to choose information on being self-employed, as well as to print out forms for sending in your taxes.

Filing Your Income Tax Return

Whether you are an employee or are self-employed, once your income reaches the minimum level for your filing status (single, married, etc.), you will need to file federal and state income tax returns once a year. This will be due by April 15th of the next year. If that date falls on a Saturday or Sunday, you must file by the next business day.

If you have never filed a tax return, you will no doubt have numerous questions about the process. Entire books have been written on this topic, and there is no way that adequate instruction can be included here. However, the Internal Revenue Service (IRS) website offers help on where to start, downloadable forms, answers to common questions, and links to other helpful sites.

- Taxes are paid from earnings either by deductions from your paycheck if you are employed, or by your payments made directly to the IRS if you are self-employed.

- Though taxes taken from your paycheck are not optional, there are things you can do to decrease your tax liability.

- Self-employment tax must be calculated and sent in to the IRS in quarterly installments.

GETTING WHEELS WITHOUT BEING TAKEN FOR A RIDE

If you live in the city and don't own a car, you can skip this chapter. For everyone else, what to drive is a pretty big decision.

A car is a major expense, and can take a big chunk of your monthly income. On the next few pages, I've addressed the different options for getting a ride. You can choose the one that best fits your circumstances. Remember that you should not be paying more than 20 percent of your monthly income toward all transportation expenses. This includes not only the car payment, but also the insurance, gas, and other expenses to operate the vehicle.

There are three possibilities for a car: buy new, lease, or buy used. Generally speaking, buying a used car is your best bet, but there are several factors to consider. The biggest question most people don't have enough time or information to answer is this: What are the financial implications of leasing versus buying?

Buying a New Car

There's nothing like a new car: the smooth ride, the great stereo, and the new-car smell. But it's possibly the worst transportation decision you can make. You pay a premium for being the vehicle's first owner, and your purchase starts to depreciate the moment you drive it off the lot. Buying a new car gets a lot of people in financial trouble.

Consider this scenario: Let's say you buy a new car, and six months down the road you decide you can't

GEEKSpeak:

"If you think nobody cares if you're alive, try missing a couple of car payments."

Earl Wilson

afford your payments. Most new cars depreciate about 20 percent in the first year.

After six months, your payments have mostly gone toward interest, not principal. So if you bought a $30,000 car and financed it for five years at a 7 percent interest rate, your payment would be about $600 a month. After six months, you'd owe about $27,500. Your car would only be worth about $24,000. If the market isn't good, you could end up selling it for even less than that. But if you can't afford your car payment, you certainly can't afford to cough up $3,500 to sell it. So you're stuck. That's why so many people stop paying their car payments and end up having their cars repossessed by the bank.

Bottom line: Never buy a new car unless you are in a very good financial position and don't mind spending a lot of money for the luxury. Some financial advisors suggest that you should never buy a car you can't afford to pay for in three years. I think that's sound advice.

 *Carefully consider additional expenses in purchasing a new car before you buy.*

GEEKOID

No matter how carefully you shop for a car, it is possible to end up with one that doesn't work correctly. To help consumers that have bought "lemons," or defective vehicles, each state has passed its own version of a Lemon Law. Check your state's law for specifics.

COSTS INCURRED WHEN BUYING

When you buy a car, you are paying for the entire cost of a vehicle, regardless of how many miles you plan to drive it or how long you plan to keep it. Here's a breakdown of some of the money involved.

- Sales Price – the price you agree to pay for the vehicle. Most people get a loan for all or a portion of this. The first payment is due one month after signing the contract.

- Down Payment – money that you pay up front. Some loan providers will finance only a portion of the price of a vehicle, requiring you to make a down payment of 5 to 20 percent.

- Sales Tax – tax paid on a vehicle at the time of the purchase. This amount varies by state. Check to see what the rate is in your state—sometimes you can roll this amount into your loan.

- Interest on Loan – money you pay to get a loan, which can range from one to 20 percent, depending on the market and your credit score.

- License Fee – money paid for a license for your car, the price of which varies from state to state. It can range from $25 for the tag only to $1,000 for tag and tax.

- Insurance – required when you buy the car. Liability insurance is required in most states, and your loan issuer will require you to have comprehensive coverage. For a new car, you're probably looking at $1,000 to $3,000 per year for insurance, depending on your credit score and driving record.

TIPS FOR BUYING A NEW CAR

If you're still set on driving something new off the showroom floor, there are some things you can do to make the wisest decision possible.

- Ask friends and family members their opinions about the cars they drive. You'll get a feel for which cars seem to require fewer repairs and provide the most enjoyment to their owners.

- Once you've decided on the type of vehicle you want to purchase, shop around for the best deal. This can be time-consuming, because most dealers won't just give you a price

GEEKOID

If you're interested in a particular car, check information from companies that regularly test all vehicles for safety, reliability, and performance, such as *Consumer Reports*. You can access their findings online for about $5 a month.

without sitting down to talk, checking your credit, and discussing a possible trade-in.

The easiest way to get the best price without wasting your time is to send a fax or e-mail to all dealerships in your area. Tell them the exact model and options you are looking for, and ask them to fax, e-mail, or call with their best price. Be clear that you are sending this to several dealerships and that you are not interested in playing games. You will usually get several offers, but you'll weed out dealers who aren't interested in someone who is looking for the best price.

• There are many websites that do the legwork for you. Type in what you are looking for, and they will send that information to dealerships within a specified radius. They will then contact you with the "best" price. Many credit unions offer this personal shopping service, as well. Talk with your local bank or credit union to get more information.

Buying a Used Car

Buying a used car is usually a better financial decision than buying new or leasing. The costs incurred to own a used car are the same as a new car, except that the sales price is usually lower, meaning

GEEKOID

Another good source for checking out a car you're considering is the National Highway Traffic Safety Administration (NHTSA) hotline at (800) 424-9393. You can also check their website at nhtsa.dot.gov.

GUERRILLA GEEK

Best Times to Buy a Car

Best time of the year: when there is a sale or seasonal clearance going on. Statistics show that these events really do save consumers money. Remember that the car year does not start in January and end in December. Spring and summer usually mark the end of their year and the start of clearance pricing. Pay attention to commercials on TV or on the radio.

Best week: the last week of the month. Salespeople have quotas for sales and profit. The last week of the month, they may have met their profit quotas, but not their sales quotas. That means they will probably drop their commission to make the sale.

Best day: midweek. Rainy or snow days can also be a good time. Sales are usually slow on nasty days, so you can get better deals.

your sales tax and vehicle/tag/license taxes, as well as insurance, will be much lower.

The only thing that likely will cost you more is maintenance and repairs. To keep those costs to a minimum, have a trusted mechanic check out any car you are seriously considering. Some used-car dealers, such as Driver's Way or CarMax, offer bumper-to-bumper warranties to cover major repairs. These are usually a good deal for those who want fixed expenses and can't do the repairs themselves.

TIPS FOR BUYING A USED CAR

So you've decided to buy something that's been previously driven. It may have a few miles on it, and some stories it could tell, but still you can get a good car this way. And you'll be getting one for which someone else has already taken the depreciation.

GEEKOID

To see if you're being offered a good deal on a used car, check with the Kelley Blue Book. It's been a standard guide for years. Headquartered in Irvine, California, it is the U.S.'s largest appraiser of automobiles.

Here are some things to consider as you begin your search.

- Take time to evaluate your needs. If only one or two people will usually be riding in the car, think small. If you're looking for a family vehicle, think bigger, but economical.

GEEKOID

Before you buy any car from a dealer, ask about the return policy. Get it in writing and make sure you understand it. The right to return a car within a few days for a refund exists only if the dealer grants it. The days during which you may return the car, called a "cooling-off period," give the buyer time to return a car that he has decided is not right for him.

GEEKOID

Once you've decided on the kind of car you want, check to see if any Technical Service Bulletins (TSBs) have been issued about it. These are advisories to mechanics that are issued when many people report the same problem with a particular car.

GUERRILLA GEEK

The Federal Trade Commission's (FTC) Used Car Rule requires dealers to post a Buyers Guide in every used car offered for sale. As outlined on the FTC's website, the Guide must tell you

- whether the vehicle is being sold "as is" or with a warranty
- what percentage of the repair costs a dealer will pay under the warranty
- that spoken promises are difficult to enforce
- to get all promises in writing
- to keep the Buyers Guide for reference after the sale
- information about the major mechanical and electrical systems on the car
- that you should ask to have the car inspected by an independent mechanic before you purchase it

GEEKOID

You can learn the history of a used car by getting a vehicle history report before you buy. All you'll need is the VIN (Vehicle Identification Number—found under the car windshield). The report will cost you about $25. For the fee, some companies offer you an unlimited number of reports within thirty days of your first report.

- Once you've realistically looked at your needs, decide which make and model will be a good fit. Then, don't be tempted to overbuy!

- Research the car to find out if there have been any problems with the make and model under consideration.

- Check dealers and the paper to see if you can locate the car you want.

- Negotiate for your best deal.

- Before you buy, have a trusted mechanic check the car out thoroughly. Make sure it has not been wrecked, and look for subtle indicators of problems.

GUERRILLA GEEK

If the manufacturer's warranty is still in effect for the used car you buy, the dealer may include it in the "systems covered" section of the Buyers Guide. To make sure you can take advantage of the coverage, ask for the car's original warranty documents. Then verify the information by calling the manufacturer's zone office.

Don't take anyone's word for the car's condition. Do not buy the car if the person selling it is not willing to let you have it checked out.

• Ask to see maintenance records to make sure the car has been taken care of.

• Test-drive the car under several different conditions.

 *A used car is often a better financial choice than a new car.*

Leasing a Car

Leasing gets a bad rap. But it can be the best way to go in some instances. It offers a couple of distinct advantages such as lower monthly payments and lower upfront costs. In particular, if you are self-employed and can expense your car on your taxes, if you get a new car every three years, and if you want to drive the best car for your buck to impress your friends and family, leasing may be for you. It may also be a good option for someone who always wants to drive a car under warranty, so they don't have to worry about repairs.

GEEK*Speak:*

"Never invest your money in anything that eats or needs repairing."

Billy Rose

The important thing about leasing is to understand what you're getting up front and compare all the costs incurred against buying new. First, realize that there are two types of leases you'll be offered.

- Closed-end lease – In this type of lease, you may return the car at the end of the lease and simply walk away. But you will still be responsible for certain charges, such as those for excess mileage, wear and tear, and disposition. You also have an option to just buy the car for its residual value, which was determined when you initially signed the lease. That, plus a processing fee will make the car yours.

- Open-end lease – In this lease, the market value of the car is determined at the end of the contract term. That amount is then compared to the pre-determined residual value of the car, and you pay the difference, which can be substantial. This type of lease is best for commercial business leases.

Gap insurance is the insurance that pays the difference between what the car is worth and what you owe if it is wrecked or becomes a total loss.

COSTS INCURRED WHEN LEASING

When you lease a car, you are paying for only a portion of a vehicle —what you will use.

- Lease price – the monthly price you agree to pay to drive the vehicle for a specified term. The first and last payments are due upon signing the contract.

- Down payment – anywhere from 5 to 20 percent.

- Sales tax – paid on the portion of the vehicle you will use. This amount varies by state. You should check to see what the rate is in your state. This tax is added into your monthly payments.

- Money factor – money paid for leasing a car, which is comparable to the interest rate to get a loan.

- License fee – money paid for a tag for your car, the price of which varies from state to state. It can range from $25 for the tag only to $1,000 for tag and tax.

GEEK Speak:

"Car sickness is the feeling you get when the monthly payment is due."
Anonymous

- Insurance – lease will require full coverage (liability and comprehensive) insurance on the car. Gap insurance isn't always required, but is definitely something you'll need. This is insurance that pays the difference (the gap) between what the car is worth and what you "owe" if the car is wrecked and becomes a total loss. You're probably looking at $1,000 to $5,000 per year for insurance.

GEEKOID

Don't be misled into signing a balloon lease for a car. This is one that begins with artificially low payments, and at some future date, you have to come up with a large lump sum payment. Most people forget about the balloon and forget to plan for it until it is almost due. Balloon leases benefit only the dealer because they sell cars quicker since they offer attractively low payments.

GUERRILLA GEEK

Don't give a dealer your driver's license number, Social Security number, or any credit information until after you have agreed entirely on a deal. You don't want to give them information they can use to negotiate against you.

TIPS FOR LEASING A CAR

Although it's true that you aren't concerned with the resale value of a leased car, you don't want to lease a car that will be in the shop more than out. Even if the repairs are covered under a warranty, having a car repaired often takes lots of time and hassle. You want to make sure the car you're driving is safe and reliable.

- After you've decided on a model, look for special lease programs, or ask salespeople if any are coming up.

- Be sure you know the annual mileage allowance each lease offers. If you drive more than the allotted miles, you will pay

GEEKOID

If you're not buying your leased vehicle at the end of your contract, make sure to return it in good shape so you aren't charged for excess wear. Having it professionally detailed is a relatively inexpensive way to make sure it looks its best.

dearly. Most leases charge $0.30 per mile or more. If you go over by 2,000 miles a year in a 3-year lease, that could cost you $1,800.

- Don't lease a car for a period of time longer than the manufacturer's warranty.

- Keep leases to thirty-six months or less. Most experts agree it's cheaper to buy the car than to lease it for longer than that.

- Negotiate everything.

- Read the lease agreement thoroughly before you sign it.

- Keep thorough records of all maintenance performed while you have the car.

GEEKOID

Here's a thought for you when choosing the color of your vehicle: some colors may be safer than others. According to researchers at the University of Auckland in New Zealand, silver cars are 50 percent less likely to be involved in a crash resulting in a serious injury as compared to white cars. Statistics have shown that the safest colors are brown, black, and green. White is the most visible at night (no surprise there), and red is as hard to see after dark as black.

GEEK AT A GLANCE

- When you need a new vehicle, you have three options: buy a new car, buy a used car, or lease a car.

- Buying a new car may be exciting, but it makes the least financial sense, since cars depreciate immediately.

- Buying a used car is a reasonable option. You should decide on what type of car you want, and then try to locate one with a dealer or an individual.

- Once a used car has been located that seems to be what you want, check for signs of major problems, and ask to have it checked by an independent mechanic. Do not deal with any seller who will not agree to this.

- Before you buy a used car, learn about its history from companies that can research it using the car's VIN (Vehicle Identification Number).

- Leasing a car is a popular option for many people. It requires less money up front, and payments are usually less than for a purchase.

- Be sure you thoroughly understand the terms of a car lease before signing papers.

HUNTING FOR HEARTH AND HOME

Should you buy a home, rent an apartment, or live at home with Mom? Owning your own home is said to be the American dream, and home ownership is a wonderful feeling, but that doesn't mean it's always the best financial decision.

Generally speaking, once you've saved enough money for a down payment, buying a home is a somewhat stable investment. A lot of financial advisors don't like to call buying a primary residence an investment—it is simply a place to live, and as long as it fits in your budget, is convenient, and works for your situation, you just consider it a housing expense.

For one thing, you aren't guaranteed a return on your "investment." For another, even if you begin to build equity in your home, it's not liquid. Chances are that if you sell your home for double what you paid for it, you aren't going to bank that money. You're just going to buy another home that will probably be in line with what you just sold or higher, meaning you put your money toward something else and end up in the same position.

GEEK*Speak:*

"No man but feels more of a man in the world if he have but a bit of ground that he can call his own. However small it is on the surface, it is four thousand miles deep; and that is a very handsome property."
Charles Dudley Warner

One financial advantage to buying a home with a mortgage is that it's not really your money you're investing. You only invest the down payment, and you use a loan to invest in the rest of it. This is called OPM—Other People's Money. So if you buy a house for $100,000, you invest $20,000, and the value increases to $140,000, you could sell and make $40,000 from your $20,000 investment. Not a bad return, although there is rarely much of that left after paying fees to sell the home. So, I agree that you should only buy a home as a place to live. If you end up making money, that's gravy.

The other (BIG) advantage to buying a home is that it will be paid for when you retire. This is really the goal, so you don't have to pay for housing your entire life.

But buying a home isn't the best situation for everyone. It sometimes makes more sense to rent, so be sure you consider all the information before buying a house.

GEEK*Speak:*

"The universe is merely a fleeting idea in God's mind—a pretty uncomfortable thought, particularly if you've just made a down payment on a house."

Woody Allen

GEEK GLOSSARY

OPM (Other People's Money): The financial term used to describe situations where you can use other people's money to make money. This includes getting a loan for an investment, like getting a mortgage for a house or a margin account to invest in stocks.

Buying a Home

A home is no doubt the biggest item you will ever purchase, so you should consider the matter carefully before you make a decision. Do not rush into this important decision uninformed. Consider these questions before making a decision:

GEEK *Speak:*

"People are living longer than ever before, a phenomenon undoubtedly made necessary by the 30-year mortgage."

Doug Larson

- Do you have the income necessary to pay for a house? There's no doubt about it— buying a home is expensive. It's not just the monthly payments you have to worry about. The costs involved to purchase a home include:

  - Origination fee (usually 1 percent of your loan amount)
  - Inspection fees ($300–$1,000)
  - Termite bond transfer fees ($75–$500)
  - Survey ($150–$500)
  - Appraisal ($300–$500)
  - Credit report fee
  - Tax service fees
  - Attorney's fees
  - Title insurance
  - Homeowner's insurance
  - Taxes

In addition to these, add on what you spend to paint, furnish, and fix up the home and the yard, and it is a major expense. You will not recoup most of those expenses when you move.

- Is your credit history in good enough shape to allow you to get a mortgage? It may be difficult, but not impossible, to get a mortgage if there have been problems in your credit history. Get a copy of your credit report by using the information in the second chapter. Review the report carefully and clear up any problems that appear there before you begin to apply for a mortgage.

- Do you have enough money on hand for a down payment and closing costs? There are some exceptions, but your mortgage fees will usually outweigh any financial benefit of buying a home with less than 20 percent down. The one exception is your first home. If you can get in a house in an area that is appreciating and pay extra payments, you will usually be okay in the long run. You can then build enough equity in that home to have 20 percent to take to your next home.

GEEKOID

According to *Forbes Magazine*, the average American house appreciates 4 to 5 percent per year.

GEEKSpeak:

"I always thought a yard was three feet, then I started mowing the lawn."

C.E. Cowman

- Are you mature enough to take on the responsibility of home ownership? It's fun moving into a new place, but the reality is that you'll also be your own landlord, and will have to take charge of routine things like cutting the grass and making your own repairs or hiring someone to do them.

GEEKOID

Advantages of Buying

- Even if your property value stays stagnant, over time your equity will build as your mortgage balance decreases.
- You'll have flexibility in remodeling or redecorating.
- You could reap significant tax advantages.
- You'll one day own your home.

Disadvantages of Buying

- Costs will be variable.
- Equity can prove unpredictable.
- In most cases, if you want to move, you must first sell your home.
- You're responsible for repairs and repair costs.

- How long will you plan to live in the house once you buy it?

Usually, you should not buy a house unless you plan to live there more than two years. There are few areas that are appreciating fast enough to cover the fees involved in buying and selling a house within two years. If you're paying cash for a house and just don't want to rent, that is an exception.

GEEKOID

When you think your job might transfer you to another location anytime soon, you really shouldn't tie yourself down to a property that may or may not sell quickly. Having to keep up a property after you've moved to another city is not easy.

GEEKOID

How much home can you afford? Mortgage lenders recommend that your monthly mortgage payment should be less than or equal to a quarter of your monthly gross income. Another factor to consider is how much debt you already have. And that doesn't mean just credit card debt. It means any other regular financial obligation, such as child support or alimony.

Another exception is if you are buying a house to live in while fixing it up to make a profit, but unless you do this regularly and know what you are doing, I don't recommend it.

TIPS FOR BUYING A HOME

If, after considering these important questions above, you think that being a homeowner is the thing for you, here are some pointers to help you sail through the experience.

GEEKSpeak:

"Certainly there are things in life that money can't buy, but it's very funny—Did you ever try buying them without money?"
Ogden Nash

- Work with a buyer's agent to help you find a home. The fees are generally paid by the seller, and the help of a professional will save you a lot of time.

- Do your homework on the area—look at five-year appreciation rates, crime rates, school test scores, and at any major changes that will be happening in the next five years.

GUERRILLA GEEK

Especially if you have children, you'll want to check to see if there are registered sex offenders living in the neighborhood near the home you want to buy.

- Shop around for a good interest rate and low financing expenses.

- Once you've identified a home that you are considering, visit it at several different times to get an idea of what it would be like to live there under a variety of situations. For example, if it's near a school, you may want to know that your driveway would be blocked at certain times each weekday.

- Insist on an independent inspection by a knowledgeable and reliable individual.

- Trust your instincts. If you feel like something just isn't right, it probably isn't.

- Do not buy more house than you need.

GEEKOID

Be sure to ask about the neighbors when you're looking at a home for possible purchase. If there are problems with loud parties or domestic situations, you'll want to know about them before you become a part of it.

- Read all documents carefully before you sign anything.

TAX ADVANTAGES OF HOME OWNERSHIP

Everyone talks about the tax advantages to home ownership, but most people don't know how to compute what the tax advantage really is. Here's a quick lesson.

GEEKOID

If you're a first-time buyer, look for special financing and incentives to help you buy that special first home.

GEEKOID

According to one source, the average new homebuyer purchases more than $15,000 worth of products and services in the first three months. This includes paint, patio furniture, new light fixtures, curtains, and blinds. Within the first year, the new homebuyer spends more money than established homeowners spend over a five-year period.

GUERRILLA GEEK

Most people consider real estate to be a great investment, but in fact, it has never kept up with the Dow over any given period. And you don't have to pay money to fix up or improve your stock investments.

GEEK GLOSSARY

PITI: Principal, Interest, Taxes, and Insurance. These four parts make up a mortgage payment. If you don't pay at least 20 percent down, you will also incur mortgage insurance premiums.

Assume that you have a mortgage with a monthly payment of $1,000. This is made up of four parts: principal, interest, taxes, and insurance. You need to break down your payment into these parts. Remember, the interest and taxes are tax deductible. Here is a rough calculation and will vary depending on your interest rate, tax rate, and insurance rates, but your payment in your first year can probably be broken down something like this:

- $200 principal
- $700 interest
- $50 taxes
- $50 insurance

This means that $750 of your payment may be tax deductible. Multiply this by your tax rate. For example, $750 x 30 percent = $225, your tax benefit. This amount is reduced each year, as your principal increases and your interest decreases.

This assumes that you have enough deductions to allow you to itemize on your tax return. For 2006, the standard deduction is $5,150 for a single person and $10,300 for a married couple filing jointly. If you don't have more deductions than that, you won't be able to write off these items. In this example, the $750 x 12 = $9,000, which is not more than the standard deduction. Therefore it wouldn't be tax deductible. Keep these figures in mind when deciding what price range you're looking in.

GEEKOID

To be sure you don't lose money, look for a house with resale value. Look at quality of construction, the neighborhood, and amenities. Check the scores for schools, safety of the area, and proximity to parks, shopping, and recreation. Be sure you know how much the property taxes are, and make sure that the municipal services reflect those taxes.

When buying a house, make sure it works to your benefit that tax year. In addition to writing off taxes and interest, you can also write off any points, or loan discounts, paid at closing. Some mortgage brokers will record origination fees as points in order to let you take advantage of this tax benefit.

Buying a home is forced savings that provides invaluable enjoyment, and in a good market, builds wealth through increased value. It provides a place to live that has a fixed monthly rate, and at

GEEKOID

Homeownership sometimes brings a profit upon sale. And its the only profit that's not taxed under capital gains. For all cumulative residential homes, the first $250,000 profit isn't taxed, and that's $500,000 for married filing jointly. Not a bad deal. That's also the reason you should save any receipts from home improvements—so you can deduct those costs from your profit when you sell.

the end of fifteen or thirty years (or whatever your mortgage term is), you own a valuable asset. Just be sure you know all the facts before diving in.

Renting

If you know you're not ready to commit to buying a house, renting may be the best choice for you. Particularly if you're just moving to a new area or just starting out, it can be a great option. It might be just the thing in these cases:

- If you're new to an area, you can rent a house or apartment for six months to a year to make sure you are comfortable with the area, the people, the culture, and the traffic.

- If you don't think you'll be living in an area for more than two years, you can rent a home or apartment and pocket the money you save every month by not buying.

- If you need a little breathing space to clean up your credit rating before you try to get a mortgage, renting might be the answer. If you can't get financing, you can rent, get your credit score up, and save some money to buy a home later.

- If you think you might need to relocate soon for your job, renting can give you the option of leaving without having a home to sell first.

- If you don't want to worry about maintenance and repair of where you live, let the landlord handle all that by being a renter.

Living in an apartment is almost always much cheaper than buying a home, and you are free of any maintenance problems. It's a good situation for anyone who travels a lot, doesn't have much cash, or can't deal with cutting the grass, replacing the water heater, or caulking and cleaning gutters on a regular basis.

TIPS FOR RENTING

• Know your rights and responsibilities as a renter before you begin to look for an apartment.

• Look for special deals on apartments, such as getting a free month when signing a one-year lease.

GEEKOID

Advantages to Renting

• Your costs are fixed, so you know what to expect.
• You can leave when your lease is up.
• There's no risk of losing equity in your investment.
• You'll be responsible for less maintenance.
• You'll pay fewer up-front costs.

Disadvantages to Renting

• You won't build equity.
• You'll have little or no say-so in the upkeep.
• You won't have the benefits of tax breaks.
• Your rent can increase each year.
• You'll never own your home.

- Be sure you like a place before signing a lease—they are binding and hard to get out of if you change your mind.

- Never sign a lease on an apartment you have not seen!

- If you may be moving soon, ask for a clause that terminates your lease with no penalty if you are transferred out of the city for your job. Most apartment complexes offer this option.

- Look for an apartment that offers other amenities that you would normally pay for, including a gym, pool, or recreation room that shows movies or has games.

- Make sure an apartment complex looks safe. Read the crime statistics and check the area for registered sex offenders.

- Inspect the apartment carefully before you sign a lease. Make sure all faucets, light switches, and appliances work to your satisfaction.

GUERRILLA GEEK

If you rent, you won't need homeowner's insurance, but you will need renter's insurance. Insurance carried by the apartment complex will cover only the building—it will not cover the belongings of tenants.

- Be sure you understand the terms for the return of your security deposit.

- Have a clear understanding of the circumstances under which your landlord will be able to enter your apartment without permission.

A **security deposit** is money paid up front to a landlord to ensure that a tenant pays rent on time and keeps the rental unit in good condition during his or her stay there. It is usually refunded when a tenant leaves, assuming everything has been left in good shape, and all back rent and expenses have been paid. However, if that is not the case, the money owed is taken out of the security deposit.

 *Statistics show that the price of rent has not kept pace with housing prices, meaning that renting is an even better deal than ever.*

ANOTHER OPTION

Here's another option you may not have thought of: What about rent-to-own properties? Many people consider renting to own if they don't have a down payment, but it's almost never a good option. The only sellers who are offering rent-to-own arrangements are sellers who are desperate to sell and can't get the price they want. That means the house is overpriced, which is not a situation you want to get into if you don't have money to throw away. Every house will sell if priced right, no matter what the defects are. If a house has been on the market for a year with no sale, the price is wrong.

Rent-to-own arrangements work like this: You pay an additional amount each month on top of your payment, with the idea being that the additional money will be put into an account to go toward a down payment when you decide to buy. If you can afford an extra

$1,000 per month, I suggest you save it yourself, and then buy a house when you have enough money. That way you aren't paying too much, and two years from now you can buy the house you want, not the one that no one else wanted.

GEEK*Speak:*

"Home is the place where, when you have to go there, they have to take you in."

Robert Frost

Living with Mom

It's not a situation most people want to be in, but sometimes it just makes good sense to live at "home" with your parents.

If you're in graduate school or trying to save a lot of money to buy a house or make some large investments, not having housing expenses can really get you ahead. If you don't want such close quarters, consider finishing out a basement or converting attic space into an apartment. You could share the expense with your parents, and all parties would come out better in the end. Starting your adult life in a good financial position is so important—if you start out behind, you may never catch up.

GEEK GLOSSARY

Boomerang kids are young adults who left to go to college, or even try it on their own for a while, and then moved back in with the folks.

The reasons young adults move back home are numerous. Not surprisingly, the primary reason is economics. Also not surprisingly, the situation has its pluses and minuses. Even though it may not be something you want to consider long-term, there are some ways you can make it work. Here are a few of those:

- Establish how long the arrangement will be for.

- Children should contribute to the household—if not monetarily, then by cutting the grass, doing repairs, or helping in other appropriate ways.

Some statistics say that as many as 40 percent of recent grads will move back in with their folks.

- The time should be productive—decide what the goal is (to improve finances, finish school, recover from divorce), and work on that.

- Set the terms both parents and child(ren) can live with. Parents should realize that these are adult children, and children should realize that their parents have other interests besides them.

- Make sure it is a mutually beneficial arrangement. Children should not expect to live without responsibility.

- The most important guideline should be mutual respect.

GEEKOID

Money (or lack of it) is the reason many young adults are moving back home. According to the Bureau of Labor Statistics, 10.9 percent of adults in their early twenties were unemployed in September 2003. That reflected a rise from 6.7 percent three years earlier.

GEEK AT A GLANCE

- Choosing a place to live is one of the most important decisions an individual can make. He or she has three options: buy, rent, or return home with the folks.

- Buying a home should not be entered into lightly. It should only be considered and pursued when an individual is prepared financially, and has the money to cover not only the down payment, but other up-front costs, which are significant.

- Renting is an option for those looking for a short-term arrangement, or those who do not plan to stay in a city for more than two years.

- Returning home can be an option for those looking to lay low while bettering their financial situation, finishing school, or while taking time to decide what to do next.

POLICIES FOR STAYING HEALTHY, WEALTHY, AND WISE

Health insurance is a must to make sure you keep your financial status stable. Even if you're healthy, a sudden bout of appendicitis or a broken bone can cost a lot and wreck your budget.

And if you develop a chronic or terminal illness, not being insured can cause you to lose everything you own, and more importantly, can keep you from getting the best treatment possible.

Individual vs. Group Coverage

The first question you will need to answer in choosing your health care is if you'll get an individual policy, or if you will be part of a group, for instance, at work. If you can get health insurance from your employer, or if you are the spouse or dependent of an individual working for a company that offers a health insurance plan, this is probably the best deal for you. These plans usually offer affordable coverage for good to great benefits, and most employers cover some or all of the monthly premiums.

No matter what policy you choose, ask if there is a "free look" clause. This will give you at least ten days to look over your policy after you receive it. Then if you decide it's not for you, you can return it, and your premium will be refunded.

Most of these insurance plans cover routine medical exams and visits to the doctor for an illness. You'll usually have to pay a copay of $5 to $50; then the insurance company picks up the rest. Any lab fees for any tests that are performed, such as blood and urine tests, or other tests such as PAP smears, are additional. Some insurance plans require that you pay the entire amount, then file for reimbursement of an agreed-upon percentage, usually 70 to 80 percent.

Most health insurance plans offer the option to add prescription drug coverage, vision coverage, and dental coverage, sometimes at no additional cost.

GEEKOID

Most experts agree that single-disease policies (such as cancer policies) are not necessary, since you probably already have adequate coverage under your regular plan.

Individual Policies

If you do not have group health insurance available, look around for individual policies. Look in the Yellow Pages, on the internet, and ask friends about their policies. Some car and life insurance companies can also sell you a health insurance policy that is managed by a large health insurance company. If the larger health insurance companies in your area don't offer coverage, they can probably lead you to a reputable source for coverage.

GEEK*Speak:*

"Money is good for nothing unless you know the value of it by experience."

P.T. Barnum

While an individual policy may be more expensive than a group policy, it is still worth the money for protection and peace of mind.

If you are considering an individual policy with an unknown company, call your doctor and try to schedule an appointment. Tell them this is who your coverage is with. Chances are they are familiar with them, and may be able to save you from a mistake or assure you of your decision.

Here are some things to look for in an individual policy:

GEEK*Speak:*

"Happiness is nothing more than good health and a bad memory."
Albert Schweitzer

- Clearly defined terms – Be sure you know what is covered, what your out-of-pocket responsibilities are for common services, what is not covered, and when the coverage will begin.

- A rescission period – Most companies allow you some time, usually ten days, to closely look over your documents and make sure that you have made the right decision. If you aren't happy with the coverage within this time period, you can cancel your policy and get a refund.

GEEKOID

Some good news if you're self-employed —if you have to provide for your own health insurance, you can deduct 100 percent of the cost of the policy for you, your spouse, and your dependents, from your income. And it's an above-the-line deduction, meaning you don't have to itemize your return to get this tax break.

129

- Non-cancelable, guaranteed renewable coverage. You should make sure that the insurance company cannot cancel your policy or deny renewal of your policy if you get sick. Unfortunately, this happens often with individuals who develop cancer or other expensive diseases, and if your contract is written with this clause, there is no recourse on your part. You want to be assured that your insurance company cannot cancel as long as you pay your bill on time and do not commit fraud.

Types of Insurance Plans

Once you've decided if you'll try to hook up with a group, or get an individual policy, you're ready to consider different types of health insurance. There are basically two types: fee-for-service or managed care. Both pay some or all of your expenses when you are sick. Here are the other particulars about each.

Fee-for--service – With these plans (which are also called indemnity plans), you can go to any doctor or provider you want, and you don't need a referral if you decide to see a specialist. Here are some other particulars:

- Premiums – This is a set fee to participate in the plan. You'll have to pay premiums as long as you want coverage, with the amount being determined by the coverage in your plan, plus risk factors that you or other members in your group may have. If you get this coverage at work, your employer may pay some or all of it, and the premium can be deducted from your paycheck.

- Deductibles – This is the amount you must pay out of your own pocket before your plan starts to pay your health care costs. If you have a family plan, the deductible may apply to the entire family, or each individual may have his or her own deductible.

Generally, the higher your deductible, the lower your premium.

• Coinsurance – Once you've met your deductible, more fee-for-service plans will pay a percentage of the remaining cost of your health care. For instance, some plans pay 80 percent, leaving you to pay the remaining 20 percent.

• Copays – Vary with policies.

Managed care plans – These plans use networks of selected doctors, hospitals, and other care providers that have contracted with the plan to provide comprehensive health care for its members. Some managed care plans require you to

Just like with deductibles, the higher amount you pay in coinsurance, the lower your premium will be.

receive care only from providers within the plan's network. Others pay for care from any provider, but offer financial incentives for using providers within the network.

Most fee-for-service plans set a maximum amount they will pay during your lifetime, or for certain medical conditions. Not surprisingly, this is called a **lifetime maximum**.

In general, managed plans are more affordable, but the tradeoff is that they usually won't pay for services not deemed medically necessary. These plans emphasize preventive care in an effort to avoid paying for serious, and more expensive, conditions. The obvious drawback of these plans is the reduction in choice for the individual. Here is a summary of the types of managed plans available, and the basic features of each.

Health Maintenance Organizations (HMOs) – An HMO is an organization of healthcare providers, including doctors, hospitals, and lab corporations, that contract with one or more insurance companies to provide their services at a fixed price. In this type of insurance plan, you have one doctor who manages all aspects of your health. This is called a primary care physician (PCP). He's also called the "gatekeeper" because you have to get his approval and referral to see other doctors. HMO plans focus on preventing illness by covering well visits, therapy, and even such procedures as gastric bypass. This saves the organization money in the long run versus surgery and other treatments.

This can be a good situation, because you have one doctor seeing all of your test results, and trying to put together the big picture so that you don't have to. It can also be a bad situation if you disagree with him or her. This primary care physician can withhold a referral to a specialist if he or she doesn't think you need that particular care. And there are incentives to the

GEEK*Speak:*

"Look to your health; and if you have it, praise God, and value it next to a good conscience; for health is the second blessing that we mortals are capable of, a blessing that money cannot buy."

Izaak Walton

GEEKOID

The advantages of an HMO are its low premiums, low or no co-pays, one doctor manages the "big picture," and it promotes a preventive approach. Disadvantages are the restrictions on seeing specialists, as well as on tests, plus the fact that they are a for-profit business—the latter can mean that the bottom line sometimes comes before your health.

PCP to keep costs down, so he or she may not have your best interest at heart. If you are displeased with your PCP, you can always request a new one among doctors in your HMO.

- Premiums – generally lowest of all options

- Deductibles – will depend on your plan

- Copays – requires copays

Preferred Provider Organization (PPOs) – Like an HMO, a PPO is an organization of healthcare providers that have a contractual agreement with one or more insurance companies. However, they are more loosely organized, giving the consumer more freedom to choose their doctor, as long as they are within the network of contracted healthcare providers.

PPOs are a blend of traditional healthcare plans and HMOs. This means that you can use any doctor you choose, but more of the services are covered by your insurance if they are in the network. If you see doctors outside the network, you'll have to pay more of the bill yourself, and probably fill out more claim forms.

GEEKOID

Advantages of PPOs are that you do not need a referral to see a specialist, and you have more doctors from which to choose. Disadvantages are higher premiums, higher co-pays, and more deductibles.

- Premiums – usually lower than fee-for-service

- Deductibles – some deductibles apply

- Copays – required if seeing a provider within the network

Point of Service Plans (POSs) – This type of plan is often called a hybrid or an open-ended HMO. The reason it's called "point-of-service" is that you get to choose which option – HMO or PPO— they'll use each time they see a doctor. POS plans encourage, but do not mandate, that members choose a primary care doctor. When one is chosen, he acts as "gatekeeper" for referrals for other doctors. Members who do not use their primary care doctors for referrals still receive benefits, but pay higher copays and/or deductibles than members who use their PCPs.

GUERRILLA GEEK

If you're enrolled in a POS plan when you choose to see a doctor inside the network, the POS works like an HMO. If you go outside the network of providers, it works like a fee-for-service plan.

- Premiums – usually lower than PPOs

- Deductible – usually only for out-of-network care

- Copays – apply for in-network care

POS plans are becoming more popular than ever before because of the flexibility and freedom of choice they provide when compared to HMOs.

All managed care plans vary greatly in benefits and out-of-pocket expenses, so be sure to read all the material provided before you sign up. Don't hesitate to ask questions about anything you don't understand.

GUERRILLA GEEK

If you do not have group health insurance available to you through your or your spouse's employer, consider joining an organization that offers group health insurance policies. Professional and civic organizations like the Chamber of Commerce, American Bar Association, National Realtors Association, or other professional associations often offer the opportunity to join a group policy.

GEEKOID

Most companies offer open enrollment once or twice a year to any employees not currently covered. Open enrollment means that you cannot be denied coverage, and there are no pre-existing conditions. This means that if you have a terminal illness or other condition, you can join with no questions asked.

To help you decide which type of coverage will be right for you, it may help to ask yourself these questions:

- Is it important for you to have the freedom to choose health care providers on your own?

- Is the cost of the services you receive the most important factor?

- Do you mind keeping up with receipts and then filing for reimbursement of expenses?

- Is preventive care important to you, or do you just see a doctor when a problem occurs?

- Do you often need a specialist? If so, would you want to be able to see someone of your own choosing?

Answering these questions and then matching your answers to the information provided earlier can help you choose the right plan for you.

Other Options

Some people in very particular circumstances may have health insurance needs not covered above. For them, there are some other options.

GOVERNMENT-SPONSORED INSURANCE

The federal government offers help with two forms of government-funded health coverage, Medicare and Medicaid.

Medicare is federally funded health coverage for people over sixty-five, some people whose disabilities prevent them from working, and anyone with end-stage renal disease. This is a complex system, but if you are over sixty-five or disabled, Medicare can

PLAN	BENEFITS	COSTS
Medicare Part A	Provides coverage for inpatient hospital stays, long-term care facilities, and some home care and hospice care.	Free for most people who have worked a full-time job for all or part of their life. Others may have to pay a small premium. Deductibles apply.
Medicare Part B	Optional coverage that pays for doctor's visits and other services, in addition to inpatient hospital stays.	Requires a monthly premium of less than $100 a month. Some deductibles apply.
Medicare Part C	Also called Medicare Advantage. Offers much of the same services that a standard private health insurance policy offers.	Higher premiums than Medicare Part B.
Medicare Part D	Prescription Drug Insurance. Medicare's prescription drug plan.	Requires a monthly or annual premium.

GEEKOID

Medicaid coverage is available to those who are blind, aged, disabled, or in families with dependent children. Though it is funded by the federal government, it is administered by individual states, who define the services offered and eligibility requirements.

provide full coverage, or complement a private health insurance policy. Medicare coverage changes regularly, so be sure you know the benefits before approaching retirement and making decisions about health coverage.

Medicaid is a federally-funded health program for low-income individuals and families. Low income is one consideration for coverage, but the program also considers assets and other resources to decide eligibility. Children are considered based on their situation, not necessarily based on the parents' situation. For more information, go to their website at www.cms.hhs.gov/MedicaidGeninfo/. For specifics on eligibility and services offered, contact your state Medicaid office.

DISABILITY INSURANCE

If you are currently employed, you may want to think about what would happen if you have a long-term illness or injury and cannot continue to work. Disability insurance would replace your income if such a tragedy occurred. If you have insurance coverage at work, you may have some disability coverage there. More about this important topic in the next chapter.

GEEK GLOSSARY

COBRA, the acronym for Consolidated Omnibus Budget Reconciliation Act, is the federal law that requires companies with more than twenty employees to allow departing workers to continue coverage in the company's health plan for at least eighteen months. The employee pays the full premium cost plus up to 2 percent administrative charges, but it is a good option for someone with a pre-existing condition like pregnancy or diabetes.

HIPPA. The Health Insurance Portability and Accountability Act, offers protections for millions of American workers that improve portability and continuity of health insurance coverage. For complete details, go to the department of labor at www.dol.gov.

GUERRILLA GEEK

The earliest documented health insurance may have actually been a form of disability insurance. In the early 1900s, many people had low medical expenses since most patients were treated in their homes. The greater threat to working people was the loss of wages when they were unable to work due to sickness. So many people purchased not health insurance, but "sickness" insurance to help replace lost income.

GEEK AT A GLANCE

- With health care costs at an all-time high, health insurance is essential to an individual's complete financial picture.

- Several types of insurance are available. The first choice you will need to make is whether your policy will be an individual one, or if you'll be part of a group.

- Next, decide what type of coverage you'd like: fee-for-service or managed care.

- Investigate the costs and choices, plus the freedom to make your own decisions about your care, offered within each plan before you sign on the dotted line.

DEALING WITH DISABILITY

For most people, the mention of disability insurance naturally brings to mind someone disabled – someone *else*, that is. People never think of this as a possibility for themselves.

And yet, one-third of people between the ages of thirty-five and sixty-five will suffer a serious disability; for roughly 15 percent of those, the disabilities will last five years or more. In addition to the physical and emotional problems this causes, the economic impact is obvious: if you are disabled and can't work, you can't pay your bills. Disability insurance provides income during those disabilities—it is essentially income insurance.

Sources of Disability Income

Before you enlist in disability insurance you may want to check around and see if you already have some forms of it that you aren't aware of.

GEEKOID

Almost half of all mortgage foreclosures are the result of a disability.

Some employers provide it. If yours does, make sure it will be enough to cover your monthly expenses, and that it doesn't exclude any likely disabilities based on your occupation or family health history. Be sure you understand all the other details of the coverage, such as whether or not it will pay until retirement age or for only a few months or years. Most cover you until age sixty-five, or until you are able to return to work.

Social Security provides long-term disability benefits based on your salary and the number of years you have worked and contributed to the Social Security system. However, this is probably not enough to continue your life at your current status. In order to receive benefits, you must meet all of these conditions:

- Be disabled for five full calendar months

- Have a disability that is expected to last at least twelve months or end in death

GEEKOID

If you're looking for a job, ask your employer whether they offer disability insurance, and consider this benefit when making a decision. But remember, you may still need your own individual policy.

- Be unable to be gainfully employed at any occupation, not just your occupation at the time the disability began.

Some disabilities you might be likely to experience could be work-related, and therefore, covered under workman's compensation.

GEEKOID

Take extra sources of disability insurance into consideration as you decide how much coverage you'll need. Also, factor in any sick leave or vacation time you could take before you need to replace your income.

Getting More Coverage

If you make the decision to get more coverage, you'll need to know that there are two main categories you should consider: short-term and long-term.

Short-term coverage kicks in almost immediately after a disability, meaning that you won't go without income for any period of time. Many employers provide this type at little or no cost. It's a common benefit because the chances of an employee having to be away for a short while is higher than the chance of being permanently disabled.

GEEK*Speak:*

"If you want to know what a man is really like, take notice of how he acts when he loses money."

Simone Weil

Even though it's free, there may be a couple of catches. One is that sometimes you have to have been employed a certain period of time before you're eligible, usually at least 30 hours per week for at least ninety continuous days. The other drawback is that it may not pay 100 percent of the salary you're used to. This is simply because insurance companies believe that to pay the entire amount might discourage employees from returning as soon as they are able.

If you've started a savings program, as I've advised earlier, the combination of savings and short-term insurance should help you to weather a minor crisis without doing much damage to your financial picture. So the remainder of the chapter will deal with the more extreme situation covered under long-term disability insurance.

 *Remember, insurance is for catastrophic events. You should have enough savings to get you through a short period of lost income.*

Long-term care insurance is very specialized insurance designed to cover the costs of nursing home care if needed for rehabilitation. Its benefits usually don't pay out until after a few weeks to one year of disability. It is usually not covered by health insurance except in very limited ways.

What Determines the Cost

There are numerous factors that go into determining what your rate will be for disability insurance. Here are some things in that mix:

- Age – rates are higher for older people, since they're more likely to be disabled.

- Gender – rates are higher for women than men. This is in part due to the fact that pregnancy is considered a disability.

- Benefit amount – policies that replace 80 percent of your income are more expensive than policies that replace 60 percent of your income.

- Benefit period – policies that replace your income for one year or five years are less expensive than policies that replace income until retirement (age sixty-five).

- Current health status – rates are higher for someone with health problems than for someone who is healthy, and thus eligible for standard rates.

- Definition of disability – A policy that pays benefits if you are unable to perform the duties of your own occupation is more

GUERRILLA GEEK

Important Tax Note: If your employer provides disability insurance coverage, benefits are taxed as income. If you purchase your own disability policy, your benefits are not subject to income taxes, unless you claim the premiums on your tax return. If you do so, any disability benefits will be fully taxable.

expensive than a policy that pays benefits if you are unable to perform the duties of any job for which you are qualified.

- Extent of disability – a policy that pays benefits only if the policyholder is totally and permanently disabled costs less than a policy that pays benefits for a partial or temporary disability.

- Type of Job – a policy for a coal miner will cost more than that of an accountant.

Other factors include whether or not you use tobacco, optional benefits such as cost-of-living increases, and any discounts provided.

Know What You're Getting

There are lots of options when looking at disability policies. Make sure you're dealing with a reputable company. And look for the policy that doesn't have so many exclusions you can't take the time to read them. Also, figure out the amount you would need (at least

70 percent of your current income) and for how long. Most people who become permanently disabled need income until retirement age, when they can begin to get Social Security payments, as well as start using their money they've put away for retirement with no penalty. Here are some other things you should note:

- Make sure you know how the insurer defines disability. Some companies will pay benefits only if you're unable to do *any* job. You probably want a policy that will pay benefits if you're unable to do *your* job. This is especially important for people who do special jobs that pay high salaries. The most common example used is a surgeon who injures his finger. He may make $500,000 a year as a surgeon, but after being disabled he can still practice medicine. However, he may make only $100,000 in a practice as opposed to doing surgery. Depending upon your skills and pay level, you may want provisions particular to your occupation.

- Know how much the policy will pay you each month after a disability. Some policies pay a percentage of your income, such as 60, 70, or 80 percent. Some policies pay a flat amount each month. A typical policy pays 50 to 60 percent. Benefits from all sources are usually limited to 70 to 80 percent. This means that if you are getting income from another source, including SSI disability or workman's comp, the insurance payout would be capped after adding in those sources. Note that most policies will not replace bonus or commission income.

- Know the elimination period, or the amount of time you have to wait after your disability occurs before you receive your first payment. The longer the period, the cheaper the premiums. You should go with a policy that starts paying after ninety days

GEEKOID

There really is such a thing as a money tree. Their botanical name is Pachira, but they're feng shui money trees. They are indoor plants believed to attract prosperity and wealth, so not surprisingly, you'll often find them in places of business near cash registers. Unfortunately, the only green stuff they really produce is leaves.

or more. This will dramatically lower your rates, and you should have savings to cover ninety days or more of lost payment.

- Find out the length of the benefit period. Most policies pay until retirement age for most disabilities, but shorter benefit periods will cost much less. Your decision on this will depend on your amount of non-retirement savings and investments. If you're thirty-five and have enough savings to retire at forty-five, you could get a ten-year policy.

- Check to see if it's non-cancelable or guaranteed renewable. With a non-cancelable policy, premiums can never be increased. With a guaranteed renewable policy, premiums can't be increased for each individual, but they can be increased for an entire class of policyholders, such as an entire state or other group.

- Policies have either level premiums or premiums that increase as you age. You probably want a policy with level premiums, unless that is not affordable when you get coverage or you

don't foresee needing disability insurance for a long period. Just be sure you can afford the higher premiums as you age, when you need disability insurance more than ever.

An individual policy provides protection for as long as you pay your premiums. Group coverage through your employer lasts only as long as you are employed, and can be canceled at any time.

- If you have a disability that allows you to work a few hours a day, you want to make sure your plan will cover the lost wages due to your shortened work schedule. Most standard policies pay out only for full disability, so be sure to ask for this feature.

- Make sure your plan covers the loss in income due to taking a lower paying job because of your disability. If you're a fireman and make $50,000 a year and are disabled so that you can no longer do that job, you may still be able to work as a desk clerk for the fire department. However, that job may pay only $30,000.

- Some policies have return-to-work or rehabilitation provisions. This means that the insurer would pay for training, modifications to your work environment, or other services that assist you in returning to work. If this costs a lot extra, it's probably not worth it.

- Disability insurance is like buying a lottery ticket: if it pays off, it's great. If it doesn't you've wasted your money. But you have to decide what the odds are for you. Talk with your insurance provider, and assess your financial situation every year. The goal is to get out of debt, save money, and eventually not need disability insurance.

Here are some things to remember as you prepare for the possibility of disability.

- Be sure you know the date the insurance becomes effective.

- Make sure your policy pays for disability due to illness, not just accident.

GEEKOID

Disability insurance carriers look closely at your income before deciding whether they'll give you coverage. If you have no income, they won't give you a policy. Why is this bad? Because some people who don't earn an income still perform a job that would not be free if someone else did it. Example: a stay-at-home mom. She is earning no income, but if she died or become disabled, her husband would have to pay someone to care for the children while he works. So, if you're thinking of quitting your job to stay at home with your children, get a non-cancelable policy before leaving your job. This is only necessary if your death would cause a financial hardship on your spouse.

- Make sure you have a free-look period during which you can cancel your policy and get a full refund. This is usually ten to thirty days.

- Check to be sure that coverage is worth the cost, considering your situation. As my husband once said, "They aren't giving away anything here."

- Every individual should consider and plan for the possibility that they may one day be disabled, either on a short-term or long-term basis.

- Many people already have some disability insurance through their employer or with what Social Security will provide.

- Short-term disability can usually be managed with a combination of using one's savings together with regular health care benefits.

- Long-term disability policies are based on a variety of factors such as your occupation, age, and general health.

- Long-term disability policies have many options and you should read carefully to make sure provisions are there that you would need.

LEAVING SOMETHING WHEN YOU GO

Life insurance is not something most people like to think about, but most people need it. Since death is not predictable, it's important not to put off this task until it's too late.

The primary purpose for life insurance is to pay off debt you leave behind when you die, and to provide for your family after the loss of your income. Your family can sell your assets when you die to help pay the debt, but it probably won't cover everything. If you're married, you probably don't want your spouse to have to sell the house if he or she can't make the payment alone, especially if you have children.

If you don't have a family, you probably need only enough insurance to pay for your funeral and to settle any unpaid debt after selling assets, such as a car or a house. You certainly want enough to cover credit card debt, since there would be few assets to sell to cover this.

GEEKOID

Social Security survivors' benefits may be provided to your spouse or children in the event of your death. Check your Social Security statement for the amount they would receive.

A lot of employers offer a small amount of life insurance for their employees at no or little cost. Anything you require above this can be purchased through any insurance broker, and sometimes through your bank, credit union, or professional association.

Different Types of Life Insurance

So now you're convinced that except in a very few cases, almost everyone needs life insurance. Let's take a look at the types offered, so you'll have a foundation to begin your search for the policy right for you.

There are basically only two different types of life insurance— term and whole life. I can make this simple; in almost every situation, term is the best choice.

GEEKOID

You do not need life insurance if:

- you're single with no debt and no children
- you're earning no income and have no children
- you're retired and have no debt
- you're independently wealthy

TERM LIFE INSURANCE

Term life insurance is a straight-forward product. It is simply a policy where you pay low annual or monthly rates for an agreed-upon amount of insurance, and you do so for a particular term (period of time). If you die while covered, the insurance company pays out the agreed-upon amount. If you don't pay your insurance

GEEKOID

Remember, even if you're earning no income, that doesn't necessarily mean you need no life insurance. Non-working parents of young children, for example, sometimes need life insurance. Even though there is no lost income, the working spouse currently has free daycare. This would not be the case if the stay-at-home spouse died.

premiums or you don't die during the term of coverage, you get nothing. It's really just like car or homeowner's insurance, wherein if you don't have a covered event, you get nothing. That's really how insurance is supposed to work.

Premium: The amount paid by a policyholder to be insured.

Term life insurance is not for investing. Unless you die during the period you're covered, you get no return on the premiums you've paid.

There are two different types of term insurance—level term and annual renewable. Either of these policies can be canceled at any time by you with no further commitment, and of course, no future payout.

• Level term premiums – These policies can be purchased in increments from one to thirty years. You agree upon the amount of life insurance you want, and you pay the same amount every year for the agreed-upon term. For $200,000 of coverage, a healthy thirty-year-old can expect this to be around $250 per year. This insures that you will still be paying the same rate at fifty as you did at thirty.

GEEKOID

When is term life insurance not the best bet? If you're too old to get a decent rate. Term life insurance gets more expensive the older you get, for obvious reasons. That's why you should get a policy when you're twenty-five or so that covers you for twenty to thirty years.

If you miss your payments and the policy cancels, you have to start over again at rates based on your current age and health conditions. Therefore, it's very important to get this coverage when you first need it (when you have children or buy a home), and keep it until you no longer need it (your children are grown and your house is paid for).

GEEKOID

The death benefit and the policy limit are one and the same with term life insurance. For instance, a $100,000.00 policy pays a $100,000.00 cash benefit if you die while covered.

- Annual renewable premiums – These policies can also be purchased in increments from one to thirty years, but the policy has to be renewed annually, and the annual rate may increase from year to year. This is usually not the best deal, unless you are unsure of your future needs for life insurance.

GEEK*Speak:*

"There are few sorrows, however poignant, in which a good income is of no avail."

Logan Pearsall Smith

Some people get this type of insurance if the amount of life insurance provided by their employer fluctuates from job to job, and they want to add to it as needed. It may also be a good option if you want to increase your life insurance coverage for a short term, like for the next four years while a child is in college, and then return to a lower coverage amount.

Beneficiary: The person or persons designated by the policyholder to receive the proceeds of an insurance policy upon the death of the insured. The policyholder can name both a primary and a secondary beneficiary.

To make sure you're getting the best coverage for your situation, have your insurance agent spell out premiums and payouts for several different scenarios.

WHOLE LIFE INSURANCE

Also called cash value, universal and variable life insurance, this is nothing more than a combination of life insurance and an investment component. If it's an investment you're looking for, go to other investment options. There are a few cases where this is the best option, like independently wealthy people who need other investment options or estate planning options, some people who are starting a family late in life, and some small business owners, but most people are better off with term life insurance.

Explaining the intricate conditions under which this is the best choice is outside the scope of this book. If you think whole life might be for you, I urge you to do your research or ask your accountant to investigate this for you. Don't have an accountant you say? Then I can almost guarantee you that you don't need whole life insurance.

Some insurance companies refer to a whole life policy as a retirement account, one that forces you to save. While it is true it will

GEEKOID

What about those insurance policies that pay off your car or home if you die? This is usually not a good deal. You're better off upping your term life insurance to cover these specific debts, instead of purchasing this insurance through your loan provider.

force you to save, experts agree that these vehicles almost always earn less interest than other retirement account investments, and the huge fees and commissions will surely reduce the amount of your investment.

How Much Insurance You Need

As I mentioned earlier, you need life insurance for three reasons: to cover the cost of your burial or cremation; to pay off any debt that can't be settled by selling an asset or paid for by your spouse; and to provide for a child, spouse, or parent.

You'll need to get an idea of how much money each of these items would cost.

GEEKOID

If whole life insurance is such a bad deal, why is your insurance agent pushing it? Because these policies pay much larger commissions than term life policies. Whole life policies cost up to ten times more than term life policies, and they also pay up to ten times the commission to agents.

To find out how much burial or cremation will cost, for example, call your local funeral home and talk with them. But $10,000 should be a good estimate (we're not talking exact numbers here).

To estimate the amount not covered by selling an asset, quickly tally the difference between your debt and the value of the assets. Things in this list would include your vehicle, credit card debt (asset worth $0), and your home if your spouse or children would sell it upon your death. If you want your spouse or child to keep your home but they can't afford the monthly payments, add the payoff of your mortgage to the amount of insurance you would need.

To estimate the amount needed to provide for a child, spouse, or parent, estimate how many years' worth of support they would need to receive upon your death. For example, a child that is seventeen and about to go off to college would only require the amount you would have contributed over the next four or five years. Even though you may not be supporting a parent now, keep in mind that they may need it later.

DESCRIPTION	AMOUNT
Burial or Cremation Costs	
Car Debt (Loan less value)	
Credit Card Debt	
Mortgage Debt	
Lost Income	

 *As you get older, you should need less and less life insurance. The goal, with good financial planning during your 20s, 30s, and 40s, is to not need life insurance by the time you retire, or even younger.*

Seven Ways to Save on Life Insurance

Since life insurance is a conscientious way to help offset your final expenses, as well as some others you've accrued along the way, what are some ways to get the best deal on it? Glad you asked! Here are seven of them:

GEEK*Speak:*

"For three days after death, hair and fingernails continue to grow but phone calls taper off."

Johnny Carson

- Don't buy from your employer. If you get free coverage from your employer, that is a no-brainer good deal. But often they

GUERRILLA GEEK

In general, proceeds received from a life insurance policy due to the death of the insured person are not taxable, and do not have to be reported. Interest from the money would be taxable, however. Some exceptions apply so consult an attorney for information.

give you a small amount of coverage for free, then offer you additional coverage at a cost. This is almost never a better deal than you can get elsewhere. Take the free coverage, and shop around for the rest.

- Give up unhealthy habits. Life insurance for a smoker is much more expensive than for a non-smoker. If you smoke, stop. This is just one of the benefits you'll reap. You'll also pay more for life insurance if you are overweight. So drop the pounds, and you'll save money.

- Buy more, save more. You get a better deal per unit by buying more life insurance. In fact, you won't pay much more for $250,000 coverage than for $200,000. Don't buy more than you need, but make sure you know how little extra you'd have to pay for a lot more coverage. You'll also get a better deal if you group your coverage with your spouse.

- If you have health problems, seek out a specialist. Some companies that commonly cover people with certain illnesses will rate your illness by level of seriousness. If you have

GEEKOID

One important note: do not lie to get a cheaper rate. If you smoke and die from a smoking-related illness, or if you have another illness you don't disclose and the insurance company finds out after your death, they can refuse to pay out and refund the premiums paid to family members instead.

GEEKOID

Keep a list of all savings, loan, investment, and retirement account numbers, as well as any life insurance policies along with contact info for the companies, and passwords so that your spouse or children can notify them of your death, close out the accounts, and collect payouts.

diabetes, but control it with diet and exercise, you would get a better rate than someone with diabetes who has to take insulin and has organ damage from the disease.

- Don't buy the extras. They are usually not worth the money. One of these is an accidental death rider, also called double indemnity. For $1-2 per $1,000 of coverage you can add this rider that pays out double if you die in an accident. This is not worth the gamble, unless you are a risky person that is likely to die in an accident before you retire. Another extra is a waiver of premium rider. This means that your insurer will continue your coverage with no premiums if you become disabled. You should have disability insurance to cover this.

GEEK*Speak:*

"Dying is the most embarrassing thing that can ever happen to you, because someone's got to take care of all your details."

Andy Warhol

- Watch for hidden fees. Be sure you know exactly what your premium includes, and question any fees. For example, if you choose to pay your premiums monthly instead of annually, you could be charged an extra 10 to 20 percent for this convenience. Instead, put your premium for next year in a savings account each month, then pay all at once. Not only have you saved the fee, but you've earned interest while doing it.

- Shop around. Get quotes from at least three sources. And make sure they are reputable sources before handing over your premiums.

GEEKOID

Rate your insurance company. Life insurance companies are rated on how they pay out upon death. You want an insurer with an A or AA rating. You can check these ratings easily on the internet, or you can ask your insurer for documentation of their rating.

GUERRILLA GEEK

The first life insurance company in the United States was started in 1735 for the benefit of Presbyterian ministers' families.

GEEK AT A GLANCE

- Life insurance is a way of making sure that your final expenses, as well as other debts you may already have at the time of your death, are paid.

- It is also a way to insure that income continues for your family in your absence.

- There are basically two types of life insurance: term and whole life, the latter of which offers several variations with particular benefits.

- Even though life insurance is a necessary, not elective, expense, there are ways to make sure you get the best deal. Talk with a life insurance agent to discuss the various plans, and which benefits and costs are right for you.

COVERING YOUR ASSETS

Your two biggest assets are your car and home. Insuring them is essential to your financial security.

Here are the basics about being sure you're covered in the event of an accident or crime.

Homeowner's Insurance

If you own your home, you need homeowner's insurance. If you get a mortgage when you buy your home, it will be required by your mortgage company. The main purpose of homeowner's insurance is to help you replace or repair your home if damage occurs from fire or natural disasters such as floods and hurricanes. The other purpose is to protect you from lawsuits. If someone falls in your home and becomes paralyzed, you are legally responsible for their accident. If your dog bites someone and does permanent damage, you may be responsible for their long-term care. While this rarely happens, and I hope you have friends who wouldn't sue you, it's something you have to protect against.

GEEK*Speak:*

"Home is the most popular, and will be the most enduring of all earthly establishments."
Channing Pollock

In general, here's what will usually be covered by your standard homeowner's policy. Check yours for particulars because they vary according to individual policy.

- The home itself – this includes extensions, like a garage.

- The outdoors – this includes lawn and landscaping.

- Other structures – this means buildings not attached, like greenhouses, pool houses, and gazebos.

- Living expenses – if your home is damaged, the policy will usually cover your living expenses if you must live elsewhere while repairs are made.

- Possessions – covers not only your personal contents, but also those of guests who were there at the time of the damage.

- Borrowed items – includes things you may have borrowed that were in your possession at the time of the damage.

There are a few other particulars that may be included as well, but those are the items you'll most likely be concerned with.

Extra Coverage

Even though the basics will be covered by your homeowner's policy, there are other types you can get that may be helpful, depending on your particular circumstances and location.

- Flood insurance – If you're in an area prone to floods or hurricanes, be sure to have flood insurance. This will be required by your mortgage company if you're home is in a flood zone (Always make sure you know this before you buy a house!). Otherwise, damage from rising water will not be covered. No matter how much extra this is, and if there's any chance of flooding, it's probably worth the extra money. Flood insurance is also offered by FEMA at www.floodsmart.gov.

- Replacement coverage – Most insurance policies will reimburse you 50 to 75 percent of what it will cost you to replace everything you have covered. This includes your dwelling, as well as your possessions. Replacement coverage costs more, but it covers 100 percent of what it would cost to replace your belongings. For example, you 20-year old T.V. may be worth only about $30, but it would cost you $200 to replace it. This is only worth the extra premium if this would really put you in a financial bind after a catastrophic event.

GEEK*Speak:*

"Where we love is home—home that our feet may leave, but not our hearts."
Oliver Wendell Holmes

- Luxury riders – Insurance companies charge extra to cover items such as jewelry and furs. It is usually not worth the extra money to get these riders. If you can afford a $3,000 fur, you probably won't be that financially impacted if something happens to it. Remember, insurance should cover big financial losses, not expensive luxury items.

GEEKOID

Homeowner insurance tips

- Review your policy annually.
- Identify risks not covered by your policy.
- Do your homework when price shopping.
- Research carrier performance.

GUERRILLA GEEK

Some things to keep in mind when getting insurance:

- Make sure you have enough coverage to replace at least the items you will need after a disaster. This includes clothing, the cost to rebuild and furnish a new house, and also a place to stay while your house is being rebuilt.
- To be sure you're fully covered, make a list of every item in your home, and what it would cost to replace the items you would want to replace. Do this by going room to room, being sure not to forget anything, including appliances, linens, carpeting, and other items you take for granted.
- It's a good idea to store your list of belongings in a safe place outside your home, like a safe deposit box. Include snapshots of your items, which will help prove ownership if you need to file a claim.
- Each year when your policy renews, review the policy declarations page, which shows limits of coverage and optional coverages. Make sure you change your coverage limits to take these changes into account.

RENTER'S INSURANCE

If you are renting instead of buying a home, you should have a basic renter's insurance policy. Renter's insurance covers the items that you own, such as TVs, stereos, clothing, or furniture. If there is a fire or other catastrophe, the owner is responsible only for his or her property, not for replacing yours. This type of insurance is generally inexpensive, and will also protect you if you are the cause of the catastrophe. For example, if you live in an apartment building and your oven starts a fire in the entire building, your insurance would protect you against having to replace everyone's belongings and having to pay for the damage to the building.

 *If you rent an apartment or a home, you must have renter's insurance to cover your belongings. The owner of the building's insurance will cover only his property—not yours!*

You should talk with an agent to get all the details, and only cover items that you can't afford to lose.

Car Insurance

Like homeowner's insurance, full coverage car insurance will be required by your loan company if you borrow money to buy a car. And in most states, liability and uninsured motorist coverage is required to get a license tag. Overlooking these two requirements, unless you're wealthy enough to pay cash for a car and not look back if it's a total loss, and can afford to pay for any damage you do to someone else's car, property, or body, you need full coverage insurance. So, here are the facts about car insurance.

Full coverage car insurance includes comprehensive, collision, medical, liability and uninsured motorist coverage. I'll break these components down to help you understand the full package.

- Comprehensive – This coverage pays for your car if it's stolen, vandalized, or damaged in some way other than a collision.

- Collision – This covers damage to your car from an accident, or collision, thus the name. Note that this is for damage to your car only, meaning that if your car isn't worth much and it's paid for, you probably don't need it. You'll have to weigh the cost of this with the value of your car. You might be better off putting the premiums into a savings account in case you have to buy a new car.

GEEKSpeak:

"The one thing that united all human beings, regardless of age, gender, religion, economic status or ethnic background, is that, deep down inside, we ALL believe that we are above-average drivers."

Dave Barry

- Medical – This provides for medical expenses to you and your passengers that are the result of an accident. You'll have to decide how much you think you are likely to need. For example, if you usually drive alone, you'd need less. If you are a parent who drives a car load of kids around all day (yours and others), you'll probably need more. Talk to your agent about the different levels of coverage and how they affect your premium.

- Liability and Uninsured Motorist – Liability covers damage you cause to others in an accident. This means damage to their car, but also covers any other damages, such as the death of an occupant of another car or yours, and any lawsuit that would result. There are limits to how much your insurance company will pay out for such damages, and it only protects you for that amount, but most people sue others for an amount they think they are likely to get, and that is usually the amount of your limit. A personal umbrella can provide more coverage. Talk to your insurance company to get all the details.

Uninsured motorist coverage will protect you in case you are in an accident caused by an uninsured driver. If you find yourself the victim in this type of situation, your own coverage will take over.

A careful look at your car insurance options can help you be a responsible and protected car owner.

GEEK AT A GLANCE

- Your home and your car are your two most expensive assets.

- Since they represent the biggest potential for loss, you should be sure you are fully insured.

- If you do not own your home, but rent an apartment or home instead, be sure you have renter's insurance. Remember that any insurance the owner of the building has on his property does not cover your belongings.

GEARING UP FOR THE GOLDEN YEARS

For people in their 20s, 30s, or even 40s, retirement seems like a long way off, but saving early is the key to living comfortably after retirement.

With the average life expectancy increasing, people are living longer and are more active during their later years. Today's retirees are looking to find fulfilling activities, to travel, and to continue to enjoy their lives. Proper planning can insure that these really are the golden years.

GEEK*Speak:*

"The trouble with retirement is that you never get a day off."
Abe Lemons

GEEKOID

Know your Social Security retirement benefits. If you were born before 1938, your full retirement age is sixty-five. Because of a 1983 change in the law, the full retirement age will increase gradually to sixty-seven for people born in 1960 or later. You can retire as early as age sixty-two and take your benefits at a reduced rate, or continue to work and delay retirement until age seventy and receive higher benefits because of additional earning and special credits for delayed retirement.

It may seem like it's hard to plan what to save, but it's really pretty simple. In your 20s and 30s, you should put about 10 percent of your income toward retirement. Just do what's easy—if your employer offers a plan, contribute to that. You don't have to work any complex formulas at this age. The important thing is just to save.

You can also take into account that your nest egg will continue to earn interest—you won't take it all out in one lump sum.

Once you reach your 40s, the picture becomes clearer about how much is enough. Most people are close to their top earning potential in their 40s, and most people will need about 70 percent of their pre-

GEEK*Speak:*

"It's nice to get out of the rat race, but you have to learn to get along with less cheese."

Gene Parret

retirement income after they retire. This is a good time to figure out how much that will be. For example, for a couple earning $100,000 annually today, they will need about $70,000 a year when they retire to maintain the same lifestyle. Assuming you will retire at age sixty-

GUERRILLA GEEK

Why will you need only 70 percent of your current income after retirement? Most people have their home paid for by the time they retire, so they no longer have a mortgage. Also, after retirement, you no longer have to pay the 7.65 percent for FICA taxes. You are no longer saving for retirement!

GEEKOID

Most people feel they have to save for their children's college throughout their life. You should never do this in place of saving for retirement. If you have to choose, save for you, not for them. College students can get a loan for their education; you cannot get a loan for retirement.

five and live to ninety-five, they will need a total of $2.1 million dollars in their nest egg.

While most people are afraid to count on Social Security, for now they should take it into consideration. If you're working you should be receiving a statement annually from Social Security telling you what you will receive when you retire. So deduct that from how much you have to save.

Annuities – This is a contract between you and an insurance company under which you agree to provide a lump-sum payment or series of payments. In return, the insurer agrees to make periodic payments to you beginning immediately or at some future date. They usually offer tax-deferred growth of earnings and may include a death benefit payable to your designated beneficiary. There are two types:

- Fixed annuity – the insurance company guarantees that you will earn a minimum rate of interest while your account is growing. It also agrees that the payments to you will be a guaranteed dollar amount. These payments may last for a definite or an indefinite period, such as your lifetime.

- Variable annuity – With this option, you can choose to invest from among a range of different options, typically mutual funds.

The rate of return you receive, and the amount of the payments you will receive, will vary depending on the performance of the options you have selected.

401(k), 403(b), and 457 Plans – These are employer-sponsored plans that allow employees to contribute a certain pre-tax percentage of their paycheck into investments authorized by the plans. Some companies will match a portion of your contributions up to a certain percentage (usually 3 to 4 percent), which is an excellent way to accumulate additional funds.

GEEK*Speak:*

"The question isn't at what age I want to retire, it's at what income."

George Foreman

- Since the money is taken from your paycheck pre-tax, it is not counted toward the individual's net income.

- Employees don't pay taxes on the funds until they are withdrawn after retirement, when the employees may be in a lower tax bracket.

GEEKOID

401(k) and 403(b) plans are both named after the IRS sections that describe the programs. 401(k)s are for employees of corporations and privately-held companies, and 403(b)s are the same type plan, but are specifically for university, church, civil government, and non-profit employees. 457 plans are also similar, and cover employees of state and local governments.

GEEKOID

Businesses must usually have at least twenty-five employees to establish a 401(k) plan. Employers should check on the requirements, since they vary according to individual plans.

- Typically, employees can contribute up to 15 percent of their annual income, with a maximum of $15,000.

IRAs – An Individual Retirement Account is a plan for those who are employed or self-employed. The most common are the traditional IRA and the Roth IRA.

GEEKOID

New for 2006! In January 2006, the IRS introduced Roth 401(k) and Roth 403(b)s. Check with your employer or your tax or investment advisor for more information about these products.

GUERRILLA GEEK

Most 401(k)s and IRAs offer a variety of investment options, and most companies let you choose where your money and matching funds go. Be sure to spread your money out in different areas. Don't put it all in any one place.

Traditional IRA:
- Contributions may be deductible the year you make them.

- You don't pay taxes on funds until you withdraw them, when you may be in a lower tax bracket.

- You must be under seventy to contribute, and your income must be greater than the amount you want to contribute. You may begin withdrawing funds at fifty-nine and a-half. You must begin withdrawal no later than April 1st of the year after you are seventy.

- Requirements for minimum opening amounts vary.

Roth IRA:
- Contributions are never tax deductible. You pay taxes upfront, and don't pay taxes when you withdraw them.

- Your earnings grow tax-free, and are not taxed when you withdraw them, but your account must have been open for five years or more, and you must be over the age of fifty-nine and a-half.

- Your income must be equal to or greater than the amount you contribute.

- There is no age limit on contributions to a Roth IRA.

- Requirements for minimum opening amounts vary.

- You may withdraw your contribution at any time, but must pay a penalty and taxes on earnings withdrawn before age fifty-nine and a-half.

	401(k), 403(b), and 457 plans	Traditional IRA	Roth IRA	Annuity
When you can withdraw with no penalty	59-1/2	59-1/2	59-1/2	59-1/2
When you must stop contributing	59-1/2	59-1/2	N/A	N/A
When you must start withdrawing	70-1/2	70-1/2	N/A	N/A
Annual contribution limit (2006)	$15,000 (plus $5,000 if over 50)	$4,000 (plus $1,000 if over 50)	$4,000 (plus $1,000 if over 50)	No limit
When contributions are taxed	When the money is withdrawn.	When the money is withdrawn.	Contributions are taxed in the year the money is earned. There are no tax deductions for Roth IRA contributions.	Contributions are taxed in the year the money is earned. There are no tax deductions for annuity contributions.
When earnings are taxed	When money is withdrawn.	When money is withdrawn.	Earnings are not taxed.	When money is withdrawn.
How withdrawals are taxed	As ordinary income.	As ordinary income.	Withdrawals are not taxed.	As ordinary income.
Penalty for withdrawal before 59-1/2	Yes.	Yes, unless the taxpayer is disabled or is using the funds for the purchase of their first home (up to $10,000) or for higher education.	Yes, unless the taxpayer is disabled or is using the funds for the purchase of their first home (up to $10,000). You must have had your account for at least 5 years.	Yes.

	401(k), 403(b), and 457 plans	Traditional IRA	Roth IRA	Annuity
Pros/Who is this best for?	Recommended if you plan to be in a lower tax bracket after retirement than you are when making contributions.	Recommended if you are self-employed or your company does not have a 401(k) or other employer-matched retirement fund. As with a 401(k), it's best if you plan to be in a lower tax bracket after retirement than when you are making contributions. You can make withdrawals at any time (penalty if under 59-1/2)	Recommended if you plan to be in the same or higher tax bracket after retirement. This is a good place for your money if you want to continue making contributions after the age of 70-1/2. You can make withdrawals at any time, and as long as you've had the account for at least 5 years and you're at least 59-1/2, there are no taxes or penalties.	You should consider an annuity only after maxing out your employer-sponsored savings plans such as 401(k)s and any personal IRAs. If you have money left to invest after that, an annuity may be a good idea. For some unemployed people with other sources of income, it's the only option. You can withdraw your money at any time.

GEEKOID

What if you have a 401(k) or 403(b) and change employers? You can either leave the money where it is, take a lump sum payment (not recommended—you will pay taxes and a 10 percent penalty), or roll it over to your new employer's 401(k) or to an IRA or annuity. Be sure you examine all these options carefully before making a decision.

	401(k), 403(b), and 457 plans	Traditional IRA	Roth IRA	Annuity
Cons:	As opposed to Roth options or non-retirement investments, earnings are taxable as ordinary income (when withdrawn). This means a higher tax rate than for capital gains. Employer contributions may outweigh this benefit. You must have earned income to participate. Some companies don't allow you to take withdrawals until you retire or leave the company.	As opposed to Roth options or non-retirement investments, earnings are taxable as ordinary income (when withdrawn). This means a higher tax rate than for capital gains. You must have earned income to participate.	No immediate deferral on taxable income. This may be offset by the fact that earnings are not taxed.	High fees and commissions usually make them a bad deal. If you need your money in less than seven years, you may pay 5-10% in surrender charges. Earnings are taxed as ordinary income, which means a higher tax rate as opposed to other investments, where earnings are taxed as capital gains.
Distributions to heirs	Taxed	Taxed	Not taxed	Not taxed

Other investments options can be grouped into one of three primary classes: stocks, bonds, or cash/stable value.

- Stocks are investment accounts that invest in companies by buying ownership or equity in those companies. Stocks make money by sharing in the company's profits, either in the form of a cash dividend or by selling the stock for more than was paid for it. Stocks don't carry guarantees, they may lose money if the company's stock price goes down, and money in stocks is not FDIC insured. Stocks are considered risky investments, and thus tend to pay higher returns over time.

- Bonds are essentially loans made to companies, governments, or government agencies. The loans are made for a set period of time and for a set interest rate. Bonds are usually less risky than stocks, and thus generally have lower rates of return.

- Cash or stable investment accounts usually purchase short-term investments such as money market instruments, bank CDs, and U.S. Treasury bills. These investments usually don't pay high returns, but they carry very little risk.

GEEK AT A GLANCE

- You should begin thinking about your retirement even when you are just beginning your career.

- When you retire, you will need about 70 percent of the income you had during your working years.

- Some retirement options include 401(k), IRAs, and Annuities.

HAVING THE LAST WORD

Estate planning is deciding how your money and other assets will be distributed after your death.

The most obvious benefit to this is that your assets will be passed on to the people you really want to get them. You will actually be able to continue to provide financially for your family by taking care of this important task before your death.

Unfortunately, many people think that their assets will just automatically go to their family members, but things you have worked so hard for your entire life may well end up in the hands of the state if you do not have a specific plan in place.

Another myth is that you have to be wealthy to need estate planning. That's not true. Whether you have a little or a lot, you need to make plans to see that it's taken care of according to your wishes. The primary instrument by which you can make your wishes known is a will.

GEEKOID

Don't count on having all your relatives gathered around a TV screen to watch a video of you reading your will. As dramatic as it might be to see and hear the deceased let everyone know who gets what, all wills must be in writing—video wills are not valid.

Requirements for Making a Will

Most people think that making a will is a legal nightmare, but really there are just a few requirements. Here are some of the most common:

- Age – some states require you to be at least eighteen years old; some states say you can be younger if you're married, in the military, or otherwise considered to be "emancipated."

GUERRILLA GEEK

Wills are required to be typewritten or computer generated unless the requirements are met for a handwritten will.

- Mental State – you must be "of sound mind." To meet this requirement, you must understand what a will is, and that you're making one, understand your relationship to the people in the will, and understand that you own certain assets that you are able to distribute in a will.

GEEK*Speak:*

"Animals have these advantages over man: they never hear the clock strike, they die without any idea of death, they have no theologians to instruct them, their last moments are not disturbed by unwelcome and unpleasant ceremonies, their funerals cost them nothing, and no one starts lawsuits over their wills."

Voltaire

- Witnesses – you will need to sign and date your will in the presence of two to three witnesses, depending on your state. They will sign themselves to verify your signing it.

GEEKOID

If you move after making your will, review the will in light of your current state's laws.

- Notarization – wills may not be required to be notarized, but in some states, witnesses are asked to sign a short document called a "self-proving" affidavit before a notary.

Although it is possible to create a simple will by yourself, it is advisable to consult an attorney to make sure you have covered everything. Particularly if your affairs are complicated by a lot of holdings, you'll want to ask an attorney to handle the more complicated issues for you.

GEEKOID

If you're thinking of making a joint will with your spouse, with each leaving everything to the other, think again. That may be a convenient way to handle property at the death of the first person, but then the survivor is unable to change the terms about the property if he or she has a change of heart. You can accomplish the same thing by making two separate wills to leave property to the surviving spouse.

What to Include

Even if you have an attorney to handle this matter for you, there are some things you'll need to think through before you turn the job over. You'll need to know:

- exactly how much money and possessions you have.

- who will benefit from your will.

- who will be the guardians of any children under eighteen years of age.

- who will be the back-up should the guardian chosen not be able to accept the responsibility.

- who will take care of seeing that your wishes are carried out after your death—that person will be your executor.

Once you've covered all the details in a will and have a copy you're satisfied with, you'll need to keep it in a safe place. Be sure to

GEEK**OID**

If you're a pet owner, and wonder what will happen to your beloved four-legged companion after your death, never fear. Now you can put legal provisions in place for the care of your beloved pet. Go to estateplanningforpets.org for information.

GUERRILLA GEEK

Handwritten wills are called "holographic" wills. About half of the states recognize this form. These wills must be in the handwriting of the person making the will, and must be signed, but they do not have to be witnessed. As a result, they are sometimes considered to be less reliable.

tell your executor, close friend, or a relative where it's kept so it can be located upon your death. Your attorney will normally keep the original and send you a copy, but you can request the original.

Assuming that your life is a long and happy one, you should review your will every five years or so, and adjust it to accommodate changes in your life. For example, if your will was written when your children were under legal age, but now they are over eighteen, you may remove the sections on guardians.

GEEKOID

Some people use their wills to make unusual final requests. For instance, Juan Potomachi left over $50,000 dollars to the Teatro Dramatico Theatre in Madrid upon his death in 1955, with the stipulation that his skull be used in the theatre's production of *Hamlet*. Gene Roddenberry of *Star Trek* fame asked that his ashes be flown into space on a Spanish satellite and shot out as the satellite orbited Earth.

- Taking care of your finances should extend to planning what will happen to your assets after your death.

- Your wishes should be expressed in a will.

- Everyone needs a will, no matter how much or how little money they have.

- You are not required to have an attorney draft this document for you, but if your matters are complicated, it should be handled by a professional.

- Care should be taken to meet the legal requirements for making a will.

- The final copy of your will should be kept in a secure place where it can be accessed when needed

INDEX

A

Abacus, 10

Annual Credit Report Request Service, 26

Annual Percentage Rate (APR), 48-50, 74

Annual Percentage Yield (APY), 74

ATM withdrawals, 62

Automobiles, 44, 93-107
Buyers Guide, 93-97
Buying new, 93-97
Buying used, 97-102
Color of, 106
Expenses, 44
FTC's Used Car Rule, 100
Kelley Blue Book, 99
Leasing, 102-106
Lemon laws, 95
Return policies, 99
Technical Service Bulletins (TSBs), 100
Vehicle Identification Number (VIN), 101

B

Balloon leases, 104

Bank statements, 15

Banking online, 20, 62, 64

Beneficiaries, 155

Budgets, 37-45, 73

C

Calculator, 10

Cash advances, 50

Cash value, 157

Certificates of Deposit (CDs), 76-79

Charge card, 55-56

Check Clearing for the 21st Century Act, 72

Check tracking, 67-68

Check 21, 72

Checking accounts, 11, 61-72, 74, 79
 Types of, 61-65

Checks
 Bounced, 31, 68
 Canceled, 17
 Electronic, 72
 Recording, 17, 64-66

ChexSystems, 69-70

Consolidated Omnibus Budget Reconciliation Act (COBRA), 139

Credit bureaus, 23

Credit cards, 11-12, 16, 47-59
 APR, 48-49
 Cash advances, 50
 Choosing, 48-52
 Fees, 50-52
 Incentives, 51
 Origin, 58
 Secured, 33, 35
 Security, 57
 Using, 52-54

Credit history, *See* Credit report

Credit limit, 58

Credit report, 23-36
 Cleaning up, 31-35

Contents of, 21-31
 Inquiries, 31

Credit reputation, 24

Credit score, 23-25

D

Debit history, 68-69

Debt, 38, 40

Disability insurance, 138, 141-152

E

Employee's Withholding Allowance Certificate (W-4), 84

Entertainment expenses, 44

Equifax, 27

Estate planning, *See* Wills

Executor, 16

Experian, 28

F

401(k), 11, 16, 41, 85, 174-175

403(b) plan, 11, 174-175

457 plan, 11, 174-175

Fair Credit Reporting Act
(FCRA), 68

Fair Debt Collection Practices
Act, 34

Federal Deposit Insurance
Corporation (FDIC), 80

Federal Insurance Contributions
Act (FICA), 85-86

Federal Trade Commission's
(FTC) Used Car Rule, 100

Fee-for-service insurance plans,
30-131

FICO®, 24-25

Financial records
How long to keep, 13-17
Organizing, 9-21
What to keep, 11-13

Flood insurance, 164-165

Foreclosures, 141

Fraud, 9

G

Gap insurance, 103-104

Grace periods, 49

H

Health insurance, 127-140
Free-look clause, 127
Open enrollment, 136
Single-disease policies, 128
Types of plans, 130-140

Health Insurance Portability and
Accountability Act (HIPPA),
139

Health Maintenance
Organizations (HMOs),
132-133

Homeowner's insurance, 163-165

Housing, 109-125
Buying a home, 111-119
Costs of, 38-39, 111-114
Living with Mom, 123-124
Renting, 119-122
Rent-to-own, 122

I

Identity theft, 9

Insurance
Auto, 12, 167-169
Disability, 141-150
Flood, 164-165
Gap, 105-106
Health, 127-140
Home, 12, 163-165
Life, 12, 151-162
Luxury riders, 165
Renter's, 166-167
Replacement, 165

Internal Revenue Service (IRS),
13, 83-85, 88, 91

IRAs, 11, 41, 175-179

K

Kelley Blue Book, 99

L

Lemon laws, 95

Life insurance, 151-162

M

Managed care health insurance,
131-135

Medicaid, 139

Medical expenses, 42, 85

Medicare, 85-86, 137-138

Money market accounts
(MMAs), 5-76

N

National Credit Union
Association (NCUA), 80

National Highway Traffic Safety
Administration (NHTSA), 97

National Payroll Week, 83

Non-sufficient funds (NSF), 70

O

Organization, 9-21
Supplies for, 9-10

Overdraft protection, 66-67

P

Passwords, 13, 16

Paycheck stubs, 16

Payroll deductions, 73

Paying bills, 9, 11, 17

Personal Identification Numbers (PINs), 16

Point of Sale (POS), 69-70

Point of Service (POS) insurance plans, 134-135

Preferred Provider Organizations (PPOs), 133-134

Profit sharing, 41

R

Retirement, 171-180

Retirement accounts, 11, 14

Revolving credit, 50

S

Savings accounts, 11, 38, 41, 73-79

SCAN, 70

Security deposit, 122

Social Security card, 11, 14

Social Security number, 15, 14-15, 105

T

Tax returns, 12-13, 17, 91

Taxes, 83-91
    Employment, 84-87
    Filing, 90-91
    Self-employment, 88-91

Term life insurance, 152-154

Trans Union, 28

Transportation expenses, 38, 40

U

Utility bills, 43

W

W-2, 16

W-4 (Employee's Withholding Allowance Certificate), 84

Whole life insurance, 155-156

Wills, 12, 16, 181-186
    Executor, 16
    Handwritten, 185
    Requirements, 182-183
    Video, 181